Both Feet on the Spiritual Path

*A Guideline to Success and
Prosperity for Christians*

JOSEPH C. PLOURDE

iUniverse, Inc.
New York   Bloomington

iUniverse books may be ordered through booksellers or by contacting:

iUniverse
1663 Liberty Drive
Bloomington, IN 47403
www.iuniverse.com
1-800-Authors (1-800-288-4677)

ISBN: 978-1-4401-3795-2 (sc)
ISBN: 978-1-4401-3797-6 (hc)
ISBN: 978-1-4401-3796-9 (ebook)

Printed in the United States of America

iUniverse rev. date: 6/25/2009

Preface

Both Feet on the Spiritual Path was designed and written for easy reading and understanding. My hope is to help readers benefit from this text by providing answers to their questions so that they can find real peace of mind and prosperity.

So, after working throughout the text, the reader is encouraged to reference the Bible. The reader will develop an understanding about ways to reach their goals in life. This book was put together for that very purpose. Having found peace of mind and prosperity, readers will be walking with both feet on the spiritual path where there is no limitation to a man who is guided by God's own words.

Reading and studying a book such as this one means we can't help but realize how great and powerful our Heavenly Father really is. The help we receive from all His blessings is ample proof.

It is a pure joy to be able to communicate and help so many wonderful people all over the world, especially in helping them gain realization that God's will is that His children all live in harmony and communicate with each other. As we do so, we also learn how to communicate with Him in such special ways that could never be forgotten by anyone.

Amen.

About the Author

The author of *Both Feet on the Spiritual Path* has been a Christian since the early 1980s. He lives a happy life in the small town of St. Georges near a river seventy kilometers north of Winnipeg MB, Canada. The author enjoys his work as a carpenter, plumber, preacher, and writer.

Joseph Claude Plourde

Contents

Introduction

Both Feet on the Spiritual Path has been written with love, with the intention of helping the reader grow in life emotionally, mentally, physically, and, finally, spiritually.

It is my pleasure to introduce *Both Feet on the Spiritual Path* to you. I believe it will help you better understand the truth about the reality of life. With that understanding, you are better equipped to help yourself and others in physical and spiritual development.

Both Feet on the Spiritual Path has been coming for quite some time. It took years of study and research, as well as discipline, thought and control (D.T.C.), to get where I am in my life today, and to have gained my understanding about reality of life and the real picture of it all.

I am very happy to have the opportunity and the ability to help you along this path so that you can start walking toward spirituality and help others walk with you, in the same direction, with love and harmony.

Both Feet on the Spiritual Path couldn't have been written without the great gift and power of love for humanity.

I welcome you to this journey with all my heart. I am sure that while reading *Both Feet on the Spiritual Path*, you will feel blessed and experience a happiness in your heart as you start developing the proper understanding of the reality of life and its purpose.

This book has been designed and written so it can be used as a teaching guide or for the purpose of study and learning. For some readers, the subject will be a reminder. Therefore, this book will help anyone working on spiritual development.

While reading *Both Feet on the Spiritual Path*, you will encounter some passages that will touch you emotionally. While sharing my experiences, you will develop an understanding that you have never experienced.

This study will help you understand and see for yourself the truth about the reality of life. It will also help you grow mentally, physically, emotionally, and spiritually. With a little dedication and effort, you will soon see that it is not so difficult to get the proper understanding. You can also put your feet on the spiritual path, with peace of mind and happiness in your heart for the rest of your life.

You will not only believe, but you will *know* that there really is a true God, and that He is very real. You will understand His purpose for you and for all of us together.

You will develop the proper understanding. You also will develop the strength you need to reach the spiritual path and walk upon it with harmony, love, and happiness.

Both Feet on the Spiritual Path should be taken very seriously because it contains very important information for everyone to use when studying the reality of life, both physically and spiritually.

It contains such importance that it should be read and studied step by step as you put the puzzle pieces together, so that you can properly visualize the full picture by the time that you've worked through it. Read it more than once, because each time you read it, you will gain a deeper understanding. This understanding is how we experience the changes occurring in our lives.

Being the author of *Both Feet on the Spiritual Path* is one of many ways God has chosen me to be His servant. He has inspired and blessed me in many special ways. I find that it always is a real pleasure and joy to do the will of God, especially when it comes to helping others resolve their spiritual difficulties, sickness, or financial problems. I became a Christian in the early 1980s, and God called upon me many times to witness to others, preaching both to congregations and to individuals for many years. I have also reverenced many people in prisons or in their homes when people had difficulties with their own understanding about spirituality. It always has been a real joy for me to do this work, and God always gave me the proper answers to give these people. I always felt so blessed, and they were also blessed. This work is still ongoing for me, and I hope it will last forever.

I have also spent many years of my life studying the scriptures and other books, of loving kindness and the like. I have visited many different churches and studied other denominations in search of the truth about why some people have different beliefs than others, which group seems to favor God the most, and so on. I also had the pleasure of experiencing many different miracles and blessings throughout my Christian life. Because of the urge I always had to help others in any way I could, I spoke to God and asked Him to help me write a book, so that I could reach out and help more people. God gave me the ability and wisdom to write *Both Feet on the Spiritual Path*, and with all the studies and research I've done throughout many years, now I have reached my goal. This book has allowed me to reach out and help more people than ever before. This was done according to God's will, because there is success and prosperity in doing God's will and not my own.

I have been working on this book for a long time. I have

worked hard on it so that it would be done properly to help any reader to get the most help from it.

Both Feet on the Spiritual Path has been designed and written in such a way that it can be joyful and easy to read and understand by anyone reading and studying it. It doesn't matter if one is highly educated, or a speed-reader, or if one professes to be a Christian, because the text was designed in a way to benefit anyone reading it.

Throughout my studies and research, I have experienced many blessings from God. I've experienced many miracles that enabled me to learn the things I wanted to learn and find the information I was looking for. Having God work with me on this project was really a true joy and happiness for me, and experiencing His great blessings was really glorifying. The teachings and learning I received throughout those years were so great. I know I wouldn't have succeeded to that degree without God's great help and blessings.

Now, because of all the hard work I've put into this book, and with the help of God, I am able to reach out and help more people in a way that I couldn't have done without Him. Therefore, He is to be thanked for the blessings that you will receive from your studies.

Both Feet on the Spiritual Path will help any reader who is ready and willing to pay attention and learn.

Anyone reading it should be happy and contented with what is learned from it.

The text contains such importance that no one should be missed or left out.

My heart is with you as you read the book's contents.

May God be with you and bless you with divine wisdom during your studies.

Amen.

Joseph Claude Plourde

Chapter 1

Opening Remarks on Development

Let me start by thanking you for letting me share all this valuable information with you.

Choosing to read *Both Feet on the Spiritual Path* is probably one of the best choices you've ever made in your life. I know you made this choice because, just like many others, and myself you are also searching for answers that seem so hard to find. You are also wondering about the reality of life, what real life is—you want to know the truth about it.

You are probably even wondering about yourself and your personality. Where do we really come from, and where we are going in life?

You are wondering what the universal field is and what it contains. What are all the universal laws, what they really are, what is their purpose, and so on?.

Like so many other people, you might be asking all kinds of questions about spirituality. Either you don't understand it or find it too difficult to put it all together. You struggle with questions about your own physical life, how it should really be lived, and lots of other things that you are trying to figure out. But you never seem to find the right answer to your questions.

You probably get frustrated at times and grow tired of trying to get some understanding about it all. You don't seem to get anywhere with your efforts.

You believe that *Both Feet on the Spiritual Path* will help you and that you will find the answers to your questions in it. You are right: you will find the answers to your questions in this text.

Just take your time reading it, and make sure that you put all the puzzle pieces together properly, one by one. Understand each piece before going on to the next piece.

By the time that you've read this text and studied it, you will have put the whole picture together. Having done so, you will be able to clearly see the true picture of it all. That is when you will find the answers to your questions, those answers for which you've been searching for so long.

First of all, this important book will be very helpful to anyone reading and studying it, so it should be taken very seriously. The content of this book is strongly about the truth, about the reality in everyone's life, and the understanding of it all.

This book is also strongly about our mental abilities and development, how we can reach our goals in our physical and spiritual lives and achieve harmony with everyone in happiness and joy. We can achieve all these things as we gain the proper understanding of it all.

I am certain that with a little effort and concentration while reading this book, you will find some very important and helpful tips that will assist with your physical and spiritual development.

First, to get to the point of realizing and understanding the truth about the reality of life, you must work with the power of love, patience, determination, dedication, and the will to do whatever it takes to reach your goal. Also, let's not forget honesty, especially honesty with yourself.

For most of my life, I have been seeking the proper

understanding about our physical and spiritual life and its development. I always had the urge to help others with matters that seem so important to them, matters that sometimes seem so difficult to understand. I had the urge to help others understand some questions that seem almost impossible to answer.

Now I am very happy to have the opportunity to offer my help to you in very important matters in your life.

Let me tell you this: I don't want to scare you off right at the beginning, by suggesting that it takes a lot of work. But I have to tell you that it does take some determination, dedication, and devotion to succeed and prosper in life. It also takes discipline, thought, and control (called D.T.C. in this text), before you start grasping the proper understanding of what the true physical life and spiritual life really are, and what their purposes are.

I like to call those powers and abilities *tools*. Without using these tools, you can't do much of anything worthwhile in your life. Without these tools, you are practically at a standstill. In other words, you remain blind, mentally in darkness about the truth of life. This book will make it easier for you to gain the proper understanding about the control of life, about how it should be controlled, from the physical to the spiritual. This book explains what we can do about it if we wish to do so.

Before we can use these tools, we have to know what they are and understand how they work. Then we work with them as often as we can, so that we can experience changes in our lives, changes within us that really should bring us in harmony with the whole universe. That harmony brings us true happiness in our lives.

We have to live in harmony with ourselves, with God, with everyone else, and with the whole universe. Only then can we live a very happy life. When we find happiness and peace of mind, we know that we are living in harmony with the whole universe and all it contains. It is then that we have found success and prosperity.

My goal in life always has been to become successful in helping anyone seeking the proper mental development for understanding the reality of life, physically and spiritually, as it should be understood by everyone.

It took me years of research and study to gain my current understanding of it all, which I needed before I could reach my goal in helping others sort out their problems and overcome those problems as much as possible. I seek to help in any way that I can, which has been my ambition and desire for most of my life,

I have experienced life at the lower level and at the upper level, so to speak, both physically and spiritually. That experience really helped me a great deal to get to the proper understanding of why certain things happens in our lives, why other things don't happen that should happen, and why people act the way they do. The results from it all, and how people react from the results and so forth, are some of the lessons I share.

My biggest hunger for many years in my life was to understand life, real life, physically and spiritually. I also hungered for the truth about the reality of life and its purpose, including the whole universe and its laws.

I wanted to understand the reasoning behind it, the purpose of it, and all questions—the ifs and whys, why this and why that, or why me or why not me, and so on.

I also had lots of questions that seemed so difficult to find the answers to, and I wasn't satisfied with just any answer. I had to be certain that it was the proper answer, and I had to understand it completely or it just wasn't good enough for me. I had to be absolutely certain that it was the real truth about the reality of life, or I just wasn't satisfied. I wouldn't settle for just maybes; therefore, I had to do more study and research to get what I wanted.

I must admit that I've been through many things in life that I surely didn't plan on experiencing. I wished neither to do certain things nor to have events happen to me, but nevertheless, those things did take place in my life. I had to deal with them with an open mind, whether it was something that brought me to a lower level or to an upper level in my life. I never quit fighting for what I believed in, and I never quit believing in God and in myself.

I've learned to have faith, true faith in myself and in my God. I've also learned that faith is the only way to survival.

My life has been a series of upstream and downstream experiences for some time. Now I believe it is time for me to share my experiences with you. I also believe that it is God's will for me to do so now.

I believe that it is God's will for me to share with you my experiences and the knowledge and wisdom that I have received from them all. By my sharing, you will also get a better understanding about the reality of life and its purpose. You also will benefit from it all, as many other people do throughout their lives, as it is God's will for everyone to do the same and live a happy life.

I have asked our heavenly Father to bless me with my mental development, throughout my research and studies, throughout all these years. I believe that He did. In fact, I know that He did and still does; therefore, it is time for me to perform my duties, as it is God's will for me to reach out and help others the best way I can. With God on my side, I know that I will succeed in helping you succeed and prosper in your life, with love, harmony, and happiness.

I know that after you finish working through this book, you will appreciate the help that you will have received from this book. You will have reached the proper development in understanding the truth about the real world and the reality of life, so that you can also reach your own life goals.

Sometimes things can get rough and tough in life, but there is always a way out. However, we must know what the right way out is and how to use it. We also must know how very important it is to stay on the right track; if we don't, we risk falling into that same old rut again, from which it is so hard to escape. But you must be serious about it and really want to change your life for the better. That's the way it should be, but there is work to be done. Remember, too, that after the work is done, there is the reward. Don't ever give up, because the reward is far too great. It's worth every effort that you put into it. You will find out and realize the whole truth about it, as you read and study this book.

Just remember that after the work, there is happiness and, with happiness, there is success.

Be strong and persistent, and determined and willing to make sacrifices. Be committed to working hard toward reaching your goal. It takes hard thinking, good integrated thinking; remember that good, hard, integrated thinking brings good solid results.

Therefore, if you want to change your life for a better life, you must make a decision, a good decision, and stick to it. To see the results, you must be persistent to reach your goal. Never give up, never quit—don't even think of it. Just keep visualizing in your mind the reward you will get after the work is done.

Keep right on thinking about success and the happiness afterward. Doing so gives you the strength and the will to keep on going, to keep striving for more understanding. The more understanding you gain, the more you want to develop wisdom. The more you develop wisdom, the more successful and prosperous you become. That is when you find real peace of mind and real happiness. It doesn't take very long until you start seeing and feeling the results.

Once you start seeing and feeling the great results, then it gets easier and easier. You keep getting stronger and happier, and you've got it made. But to reach this point, you must start sometime, somewhere. There is no better time than right now, right where you are.

Almost all of us think that it is so hard to do, there is so much work to be done, and we don't know how to go about it. Or, perhaps some people tried something before, but it never worked, and so forth. Well, maybe they don't know how, or maybe they don't really want to know how because they don't really want to change their ways or their habits. Maybe laziness is the cause of resistance. There can be all kinds of excuses, and sometimes they can be very convincing. But we have to remember that the easy way isn't the best way, because we know that, most of the time, the easy way is the wrong way. People usually like to take the wrong way, simply out of habit, because it is the lazy way, whether they profit from it or not. It just doesn't matter to them, because it is the way they have always done it and they don't want to even bother trying any other way. They are afraid a change might be too hard to do or too difficult to handle. Or, the new way might demand discipline or hard mental work, and they are afraid to try something new, something different, because they are scared. They are scared that they might have to change some of their ways. Therefore, these people keep on struggling and live in poverty all of their lives. Yet, still they wonder why they can't get anywhere worthwhile in their lives, and they think that they are just unlucky.

All this resistance is very sad to see. It really bothers me to see how people's lives can be just a struggle, and yet could be changed so easily to a much better and much happier life, if only they would just stop and think about what it takes. All it takes is to realize what to do, recognize the problem, and identify what caused the problem. One must be very honest about it and do whatever is necessary to solve that problem. It is not as hard to do as people think it is; it only takes honesty, especially with oneself. Once you find that honesty and work with it, you find that it is much easier to get the proper control in life.

It is very easy. Let me give you a small example, just for a start, and you will understand what I am saying.

Stop reading for just a moment, and close your eyes and think a kind thought about someone else. Think about all the love that you have and that you could share with anyone else. Think about how happy it makes you feel when you see someone else happy, and think about how you want to spend the rest of your life happy, loving, and kind to everyone. Ask our Father in heaven to bless you and help you reach your goal. Be truthful about this request in your heart, mind, and soul, and thank God for His blessings. Ask His help for your achievement, believing that He has already blessed and helped you, and let it be done. By believing, "your faith has made it happen." It is God's promise to all His children, and there is no mistaking it: all it takes is to "believe it," "do it," and "let it happen."

Stop reading now, and try it for a while. I am certain that you will receive a good feeling inside, a feeling that you will want to keep forever. That's where it all starts; do it now.

Sometimes, we wonder why things are going so slow. It seems as if nothing goes right, we have the feeling of being stuck, stuck in bondage of some kind, and we can't succeed or prosper. We get sick and tired of not being able to get anywhere in life. We feel as if our health is not very good after a while; we feel weak.

We have financial problems. We have a hard time making ends meet. It seems that we are always struggling. We worry about our bills that are coming at the end of the month; we don't know if we will have enough money to pay the bills when they arrive. We get frustrated and lose faith in ourselves. We are scared and don't really know what to do about it. We can't come up with any answer. Sometimes we look for an answer that could help us, but we can't find the answer that we seek.

Life gets harder as the days go by. We grow nervous. Sometimes we feel like giving up on life, because it seems too difficult to handle.

Then something happens that brings our morale up, and we feel a little happier for a while. That happiness allows us to make it through another day, a week, or a month. Things are going better, and we are feeling better. We feel a little more energetic, and we feel like trying harder or trying something new, something different. We start thinking more positively about life.

Sometimes we are fortunate enough to find a job that pays well, and things are going much better while that job lasts. Sometimes it is a long-lasting job, and we really feel glorified, really feel that we've found happiness. But, unfortunately, some of us are not so lucky and go on struggling for long periods of time. We just don't seem to be able to find any way out of this misery, even when we see others escape.

Well, let me tell you the truth about this situation. To my knowledge, the biggest part of the problem comes from the fact that most of us don't have enough faith in ourselves. We will be talking about that lack of faith later. But, before we do, there are other areas of our lives that need to be brought to the open and dealt with first.

Before we go any further, I would like you to stop reading for a while and concentrate on what you've read so far. Please take your time and think about these ideas, over and over. Make sure that you properly understand what we've been talking about before you read any more.

There is no point in reading any further if you don't properly understand what you've already read. If you feel that you need to, please go back and read again from the beginning. You will find that it is much easier to grasp the proper understanding, after you've read it the second or third time. Even if you think that you understand it all, it is always helpful to read it again.

Please stop now.

I must ask you to be patient with me. You will probably realize that some words and tools, as we call them, will seem to increase in power as you get deeper into your study. I know that some words that don't seem to be very important, but we really think differently about them after we realize how powerful they really are.

Now, we know that no one should have to go through all of their life struggling. God doesn't want us to go through life struggling. Therefore, the problem isn't with or from God; it is with and from us. When it comes to intelligence and wisdom, the truth is, we are a weak nation. We must recognize this weakness, accept this fact, and deal with it in a strong and positive way. We must get out of this rut, and to get out of this rut, we must change negative thinking to positive thinking—and stick to it. Think positively about anything or anyone who crosses your mind. Practice being alert to anything or anyone that comes to your mind at anytime. Endeavor to be positive. It doesn't matter where you are or what you're doing. This determination and practice will become a success in this matter.

Once you've recognized and accepted the fact that you truly are the cause of the problem, then you can start using the tools that we've talked about earlier. These tools can and will create a better and happier life.

We must be open-minded and accept the fact that the truth about the problem and our lack of honesty with ourselves are the key factors in our lives. Even if it is difficult sometimes to admit, even to ourselves, that we are not the smartest people in the world, we surely can admit to ourselves that we can try our best, and that is all any person can do. If we are trying our best and are at least honest about it, honest with ourselves to start with, then we are growing, growing mentally. Without honesty, there is nothing; we can't get anywhere worthwhile. First of all, keep on thinking about honesty, because honesty will bring you happiness and success in your life.

Honesty with oneself is a very big start toward happiness, prosperity, and success in anyone's life. Once we have achieved honesty with ourselves, then we can be honest with others as well. Before we know it, people are starting to recognize us as honest people, and we can see and feel that these people start showing us more respect. It seems that they want to get closer to us, that they want to become better friends than ever before.

Well, at first it seems, as we say, too good to be true. But, after a while, we realize that it is reality. It is so wonderful, and we feel so good about it, that we don't want it to ever stop. This is true happiness that we feel, and because of this happiness, we feel strong and joyful. If we stop for just a moment to reflect, we realize what we've done to bring all this joy and happiness to ourselves and to others also. We just want to do more of the same love sharing, and we want to work more on our honesty, as well as kind thinking about everyone else. We don't want to stop growing in harmony and happiness with the world around us, because our whole life has changed for the better. This way of life gives us such a wonderful feeling about ourselves that we finally start having faith in ourselves. We also begin to realize that there really is a God and that He loves us very much. We realize that He is always by our side, always ready and willing to help us if we just call on Him and let Him help us.

In the stage where we are today, we like to think that some of us are luckier than others, some of us are never lucky, and some of us are sometimes luckier than at other times, and so forth. However, let me tell you this: luck might sometimes mean something great to some people, but for others, luck just means nothing at all. To these people, reality means everything, and that is because some people do have a better understanding about the reality of life. These people do have some control over their lives, because of their understanding about life and, with a little effort, they do find harmony, happiness, and success in their lives. Other people see them and wonder how they do it, or wonder why some people seem to have success so easily when they, themselves, don't seem able to do anything right. They just can't see any way that they could become happy and successful like those people. But all it takes is to live in harmony with everyone else, realize the love that we have to share with others, and share it freely with anyone. We must also be honest with society and have faith in ourselves and faith in our God.

As I've mentioned earlier, without the proper understanding, a person is living in darkness or is mentally blind about the truth of what the reality of life really is. Others can see and feel happiness and experience success, and it seems so easy for them.

Understanding reality is one of the main points in our lives. If we don't understand what reality of life really is, and how to live according to that reality, then we could struggle throughout our whole lives and never really understand why. But if we can focus on the truth about reality of life, and understand what it really is, then we start to see what the real problems are and where they came from. When we understand what causes those problems to come into existence in our lives, then we can get the sense of how to overcome those problems.

Get rid of those problems that keep us at a lower level of living by defining the cause of those problems and conquering them. The best tool to use to conquer any negatives in our lives is honesty, starting with honesty with oneself and then with the rest of society.

We must understand that sometimes it is very difficult to

recognize a problem just because it is too close to us, so close that we can't see it. We are the cause of the problem, and sometimes, we just don't want to see it because we are scared to see it in ourselves. Other times, we are afraid of what we might find in ourselves because we don't know how we would deal with it. Sometimes, we don't even want to think about it because we are scared to recognize it in ourselves. So we think that the easy way out is to try to bypass it, just try to ignore it, and make ourselves believe that things are going to get better on their own. But that is one of the biggest mistakes anyone can ever make. The only way to get rid of a problem is to recognize it and deal with it with honestly. Conquer problems even if it means exercising some discipline, even if it means getting rid of the problems that have kept you down and kept you struggling in your life until now. Start living a happier and a more successful life. Just think about it for a moment, and be honest about it, especially with yourself, and you will realize that a change in your life is worth all the efforts that you are willing to put into it.

Remember that the more difficult it is to recognize it, face it, and deal with it honestly, the greater is the reward. Anyone who is willing to do just that deserves all the rewards. You can't fail.

Honestly speaking, problems are created by us, not created by God.

In the spiritual world, there are no problems. Problems only exist here on Earth, in the physical world, because human beings create problems—maybe even more today than ever before now. That's because people are becoming too self-righteous, and they seem to think that they can control the world they live in and the universe surrounding them. They seem to forget about God the Father and Creator of it all, from where all goodness comes.

We must realize that we cannot control anything except with the help of God, who is the creator of all, He controls all of His creations, but He also gave us the right to control His creations. If we let Him into our lives and work with Him, He will show us how to do it the proper way.

I understand that God created us as perfect beings, and if we are not perfect or are not living a perfect life today, it is certainly not God's fault. It is because we, as a weak nation, choose to live an unperfected life, because we believe that it is too difficult to be perfect. We always choose the easy way out, and the truth is *the lazy way out*. There is no prosperity or success that comes from laziness; laziness just creates more problems than we can handle. The more problems we have, the weaker we get.

Our planet, Earth, and the entire universe were created for us all, to use and to profit from, and succeed and prosper in. It was all put together in perfect accord for us, to live in harmony with it all and with everyone equally.

This is God's plan for us. But because we are a stubborn nation, we refuse to live according to God's plan. Therefore, that leaves us with the answer: that we are the true creators of our own problems. God did not create them. We must remember that if we have problems, it is not because God left us behind, it is because we left Him behind. We didn't want to bother Him. He can't help us because we don't let Him. Some of us don't even want to have anything to do with Him, because we don't like to live according to His law. We find it too difficult to follow, so we take the easy way out; usually, the easy way out is the lazy way out, the wrong way out, whether we want to admit it to ourselves or not. It is the truth, and we have to deal with it as it is.

Let's face it: sometimes in life, we must stop for a moment

and just take a good look around us and at ourselves. We must realize how we think and how we should think about what is real in life. When we do, we realize how often we contradict ourselves, and we don't even realize that we are doing it. Yet we try to control our lives ourselves, without thinking of God for even a moment, even though He is the Father and Creator of all. We even forget about Him completely sometimes, even though He is our everlasting Father. But when we get ourselves into deep trouble, then we think about Him, then we remember that there is a God, who can and is always ready and willing to help us. Unfortunately, after we are out of trouble, then we forget about Him again, until the next time we get ourselves into deep trouble, and on and on.

Now going back to our own contradiction, here we are creating our own problems and yet believing that only God can create. Well, that makes us wonder what the reality of life really is, what creations really are, who created them, and for what purpose, and so forth.

Well, as much as I know, all that God created was good and God was pleased. It was created for all of us equally, for our benefit.

He didn't create all that He created for Himself. I don't believe that He needed anything or really had to do anything. He did it all for all of us equally so that we could live in happiness and harmony with each other.

Creation includes all the great gifts and abilities that God gave us, to use and to share with each other equally, so that we could have a happy life together in harmony, with each other and with God our Father. It is His plan. It is His will that we follow His plan and that we live according to His will. But it is up to us to make the proper decision, which is to walk in God's plan and live according to His will at all time. Anyone who is ready and willing to live according to His plan is truly a wise and blessed person.

Anyone who has wisdom is a person who lives in harmony. Such a person can't help but succeed and prosper in life with true happiness.

Let me name just a few of the gifts, powers, and abilities given to us by God, to use in our lives so that we may enjoy a happy life: love, honesty, goodwill, forgiveness, kindness, joy, prosperity, success, harmony, control, discipline, patience, and so on. All these gifts are there for us to use and to profit from, only if we will to do so. But if we don't use these qualities in our lives as they were meant to be used, then we can't put the blame on God or anyone else for our unhappiness or lack of fulfillment. Therefore, that leaves us with no choice but to take the blame for our own problems, failures, and struggles in life.

If you don't understand what the word *will* really is and what it means, or the words faith or wisdom, or the truth about believing and so forth, then I strongly suggest that you don't just look in your dictionary for an easy explanation. I strongly suggest that you study your Bible, and then you will honestly get the real and proper explanation. Studying the Bible is the proper way to understand what it all means, and by studying your Bible, you should have no problem understanding any of those words or their strength, abilities, and purpose. At the same time, you will also learn more about yourself, about the rest of society, and about the universe and the purpose of it all. Remember that it is God's plan. I know that you will be very happy to discover the truth about the reality of life, and you will see the whole picture and understand it all.

Now, we know that all that is good in this world is to be shared with everyone equally. Sharing is not just *if I feel like it*, it is a must, and it is a must because it is a universal law. God's law is here to stay, and no one has the ability to change it. That is the way it should be, because it is for our own benefit and for the benefit of all society equally.

We should also know that if we refuse to share all that is good for humanity with everyone equally, then we have a problem. It is a problem that we have created, or that we are creating, and it is certainly not the will of God for us to create problems. It is certainly not His law.

Love, forgiveness, joy, happiness, success, prosperity, and so on, are all to be shared with everyone equally. That is God's universal law.

Let me give you an example. *Love* is not something that we humans created. It is the greatest gift and power that anyone could ever have. It is completely free for us to use and to share freely with anyone and everyone.

We didn't have to buy love, we didn't have to work for it, and we didn't have to trade it for something else. Love came to us free. That makes me wonder sometimes: why does it seem so difficult for someone to share love with someone else? After all, love is free, it was always free, and there is plenty of it. It doesn't cost anything to share it with anyone, but for some strange reason, people refuses to share it with each other. We refuse to share love, even though everyone has an equal amount, and we know that it is the will of God for us to do so. Why don't we do something good in our lives, with something that we have received free of charge, instead of creating problems, for ourselves and for the human race?

When someone shares the power of love and happiness freely with anyone else, this person is bound to be successful. There is no mistake about it, because the fact is that the more we give, the more we receive. When we give, we can't help but receive.

Therefore, since it is free and we all have the same amount, then why not share it freely with each other? Why not have everyone succeed in life, with harmony, joy, and happiness as it was meant to be?

We all know that it is a hard question to answer, because humanly speaking, we can't decide for someone else, even though we would like to sometimes. We can't and shouldn't even attempt to do that, and someone else wouldn't want us to decide for him or her, either. I don't think that we would like anyone else deciding our future for us, either.

We can be willing to follow God's law and do His will, as many of us do. It should be a pleasure and honor to share these great qualities with anyone. We know that God is very pleased with us. However, if the next person refuses to do the same for someone else, well, there isn't much we can do about it. We can't decide for anyone else, but we certainly can decide for ourselves. There is nothing anyone else can do about our choices, either. However, we can always help anyone else by praying for them.

But, the fact of the matter is that we can't or shouldn't even try to force someone else to do what we think that person should do, or try to force that person to do something differently, just because we think we know better. Even though we may think that they should do it our way, and we certainly can help someone else make better decisions through advice, we should not tell someone else what to do. We cannot live their life for them anymore then they could live our life for us. Therefore, it is proper to give good advice and then let them make their own decisions. If things don't go as expected, then you would not be to blame. Your good advice should be remembered, and perhaps used in the future, because I do not believe that any good advice is ever lost.

This advice I am referring to is for adult-to-adult relationships and not for parents while they are raising children. We all know that parents must make decisions for their children until they are old enough to make their own decisions.

After they are old enough to make their own decisions, then we should let them make their own, but we certainly can help by offering advice and sharing our experience. We can only hope that they will accept and use our counsel for their own benefit.

But going back to adult-to-adult communication, we can't decide for anyone else, but we certainly can offer our help in whatever way possible. We must remember to be patient with them. In fact, showing patience can be very powerful and can sometimes help a lot more than words.

Patience can be shown by sharing love and laughter, or happiness and joy, with anyone, and showing that we really care and are willing to help in any way we can—if they allow us to help. When we approach someone else with a warm smile, love, tenderness, and kindness, it is very hard for anyone to refuse our help and support. Therefore if we approach anyone in this way and with these loving qualities, and they accept us because of the way we approach them and they feel comfortable with us, then we have won another friend, found another brother or sister, someone who will trust us and who we can trust as well. This behavior is progress in our lives, and it brings happiness, success, and prosperity. These rewards are because we have been using the power of love to reach someone else, and with the power of love in action, we cannot fail. The result is overwhelming with success and happiness. This is really living.

At this point, I would like you to stop reading for a moment, relax, and concentrate on what you've read up to this point. If you have any problems understanding or remembering what you've already read, then I suggest that you go back to the beginning, read the topic again, and make sure that you understand it properly before you read on. It will be much more beneficial to you. I strongly suggest that you read the chapter very carefully from the beginning up to this point. I know that it will be much easier for you to master the understanding you need, and it will make it much easier for you to understand the remainder of the book as you read on.

Please stop now, and think about the message for a moment before reading it again.

Close your eyes and while relaxing, repeat the word "God" ten times slowly. Realize that every time that you say it, you're not the same afterwards. The degree of change is very small, but very real.

Therefore, the truth is, it is not the fault of a successful person if someone else is poor, and it is not the fault of a poor person if another is successful. It is that some of us realize what the reality of life really is, while others are really not aware of it or don't understand it the way it should be understood.

Unless you are willing to use the tools, and those great

qualities that we've talked about earlier, and put them into practice in your life, to grasp the proper understanding, then you are to stay behind and struggle through life, just for the lack of understanding of the real world and reality of life, physically and spiritually.

What a beautiful thing it would be, what a joy, what an harmony among all the people in the world, what a reunion, what a happiness among men, if we all had divine wisdom and intelligence that we would share with everyone equally. We would be living without the problems that we are living with now in our lives. It could be ever so well done, if only people weren't so stubborn, and if people were more willing to listen, obey, and live according to God's law. If we were to follow His plan the way we should, instead of always taking the easy way out with our diseases of laziness, selfishness, and stubbornness, we would be problem free. These diseases prevent us from grasping the understanding that we need and from realizing the truth about what the reality of life really is. We could cease the creation of our own problems that plague us every day of our lives, if only we were to rely on God's law.

We have to develop a mental ability, so that we can understand the reality of life as it is. Only then can we start visualizing what spiritual life really is.

You might find some of this writing a bit disturbing at times, but I ask you to be patient with me. I also ask you to open your mind to what you are studying so that you can grasp the proper understanding of what we are discussing. Remember that a little effort can be a big help to your ability to reach the proper understanding of it all so you can achieve your goal.

I believe that the best way is to deal with the truth face to face with honesty, in your mind, heart, and soul. But because we are a weak nation, we must use disciplinary actions, and those actions take practice, sometimes lots of practice. Nevertheless, it is very rewarding, as you discover after a short time of mental work (D.T.C.), dedication, and practice.

Don't worry about a little work, because it pays off. More work pays more, because the more you practice, the better your performance gets. Soon you really start feeling better about yourself. It is when you start gaining strength and happiness, and start having control of your life, that you feel proud of yourself. After a while, you feel as if nothing can stop you, and you are on your way to success, prosperity, and happiness. There is no looking back for anything in your life.

It may seem a little difficult at first, but it isn't truly so difficult; it's simply a new skill that needs to be mastered. Try it and don't give up; just keep pressing on, and before you know it, you will feel a change occurring inside yourself. You'll sense a very good and happy feeling of strength building up inside. Once you start getting those wonderful feelings, you will never want to give them up or go back to the way you lived before.

Everyone will see the changes in you, and they will be happy to see and feel the true love and happiness shining and flowing from you. There is no better way to share love and happy moments with people you meet, and with the world around you. We know that the power of love is the grand master key to harmony, success, prosperity, and happiness in anyone's life.

We know that if we share the great gifts of love and happiness, with the world around us in harmony with everyone, that everyone will love us in return. People will want to be our friends forever, because they also feel this happiness inside of them. They love you for it, because you're the one that put this happiness inside of them. They could be ready to go out of their way to do anything for you, because of what you've done for them and how good you've made them feel. At this point, you deserve to get all the recognition and rewards that are coming to you, including your new friends.

The great feeling inside of you just keeps on growing, stronger and stronger—it just won't quit! Life keeps getting better and better, every step of the way, because you feel joyful and happy. You also have peace of mind, because you develop faith in yourself and in our heavenly Father.

Just remember that true love is the greatest power of all, and if you use it properly, then you can't help but prosper. When you prosper, you also succeed in all areas of your life.

But remember that the more you give, the more you receive. When you give, you experience the happy feeling of giving or a happy feeling because you are helping someone else, someone who was in need of your help. You don't experience happiness because you expect anything in return, but because you enjoy helping someone else and you enjoy seeing someone else happy. Recognizing the fact that you've done it by sharing the great gift of love and happiness with someone else makes you all the happier.

We have to realize that giving doesn't always mean giving money, food, or clothing, or even giving someone a ride somewhere. Many times, all a person needs is a touch of love. Talking kindly to a person can change his or her life forever. Often, a person only needs someone to talk to, someone they can trust and share their problems with, and someone who is willing to listen. This kind of giving can be worth more than all the money in the world. When you see and feel the change in this person, and you recognize the fact that you've made this person happy, you can't help but be happy with yourself, for what you've done for this person.

You want to keep doing more, with not only this one person, but also you want to share the same things with others also. When you are at that stage, then you know that you have become a different person, a better person than you once were, because you know that you are doing the will of God. You are working in His plan, and you feel honored to do God's will. You also know that by doing His will, He is happy with you, and if God is happy with someone, He helps this person succeed and prosper. It has been proven time and time again. It is also a promise that will never change.

If you have willingly given from your heart, to someone who needed your love and kindness, to change that person's life for the better, well, let me tell you, it is really something to be proud of, and happy about doing.

Bringing joy into someone else's life brings more joy in your own life also. So, as we've said, the more you give, the more you receive. You can't help but get much more in return, and by now, we know that joy and happiness means success and prosperity.

The satisfaction you get from your own actions makes you feel better about yourself, you start having faith in yourself, you feel happier and stronger, and then you start experiencing success and prosperity in your life. Just keep working at it, keep pressing on, and the more you practice, the better and easier it gets. Believe me, when you feel it happening, you don't want to quit, because giving is the greatest feeling one can ever have. The *feeling of success* means a great deal to anyone else in the person's life, as well as for you.

Realize that when you experience this feeling and this kind of reward after sharing something good with another person, then you know that you have someone on your side in your life. Even though we know that God is always with us, we also get to know that there is someone else also on our side, too, and that certainly is a great feeling to realize. That someone else is the brother or sister we brought into our life by sharing the great gifts of love and happiness. We all know that fellowship makes our lives much happier and easier, and we know that we are not alone. If we are not alone with our problems or our good fortunes, and we realize that, then we automatically realize that we are living a much happier life. We get the sense that we are living in harmony, with everyone else living the same kind of life as we are living.

Look at it this way: people who don't share anything with anyone else are living alone and are not in harmony with others; therefore, their chances of success are very slim because they lack anyone to help them succeed with anything. But people who share with others are wise, because they know that it is much easier to succeed when others are helping and getting help from others comes from helping others to begin with.

There is some old saying that one should take care of himself and not worry about anyone else. But when it comes to the reality of life, this statement couldn't be further from the truth. We all know that, as human beings, we are all living together in the same world, in the same universe, and that makes us all one big family, a family of brothers and sisters. What should brothers and sisters do? Well, share and share alike. This is also God's universal law, and no one can change it. If anyone should try, he will fail.

If I succeed, then I want my brother to succeed also, so I should help him succeed in any way I can. It should also be the same the other way around, that my sister should help me. If it is done this way, then there is no mistake: everyone succeeds.

Caring enough for others to share anything with them is the key to success in the real world, and anyone who knows and understands that concept and lives accordingly is a very wise person. There is no doubt that this person will succeed and prosper in life, and it all comes from sharing love, good fortunes, laughter, happiness, and even problems. It all works in the same sequence: share with others and others will share with you too: keep everything to yourself, and others will keep everything from you too. Therefore, share happiness with others, and they too will share happiness with you, every chance they get. You can be certain that they will be happy to share with you in return.

Now, if we realize how many more rewards we can experience, just by doing the same thing with more people, then the more we share problems or good fortunes with, the bigger the rewards. It keeps growing and growing until it overflows with success, prosperity, and happiness for everyone. Make no mistake: this is just the way it is. It is a universal law, and it cannot be changed because it is also God's will, Amen.

We have to keep in mind, at all times, that good makes good and bad makes bad. So, we should keep thinking, kind thoughts, and loving thoughts about others. As we know, that is something not so easy to do, because our good thoughts slip away from our mind, and something else creeps in. More often than not, what creeps in is something that we don't really want to think about: but, before we realize it, the bad thought is already there, replacing that good thought. Sometimes, a negative thought tries to replace a good and positive thought. When we realize what is happening, we can act to stop this kind of thinking and go back to the good and positive thinking, especially when a negative thought about someone else has entered our minds. We really want to get rid of that kind of negative thinking, so we must reject it as soon as we realize it, then go back to the good positive thinking and try to stay with it.

After we realize that negativity will slip into our mind, we must be very alert to our thinking. Whenever we try to think about something good for others, then we should keep a close watch on our thinking and stay alert for slips. After correcting our thinking a few times, it starts getting better. It gets easier as we practice it, and the more we practice it, the better and easier it gets. It feels good inside, and the more often we practice this kind of good thinking, the less chance the bad thoughts will have to enter our mind, and interfere with our good and positive thoughts.

Simply go back to the positive thinking, and try to focus on those thoughts for as long as you can. Don't give up, keep pressing on and practice, and you will soon see that you are conquering the problem. The more often you work on this skill, the sooner you master it, and the stronger you grow from your efforts.

To achieve mastery, be determined and persistent. It takes self-control and discipline to conquer such weaknesses. But by using these abilities that we call tools, you develop strength and understanding about the real person inside of you. In other words, you get to know yourself better than you ever did before, you get to know a different you, and you discover that you are a better and stronger person that you thought you were. You feel better about yourself, and you start having more faith in yourself, which is a major point to succeeding and prospering in life.

This is one of the key puzzle pieces we must find in our lives, and we must work on it, with as much practice as possible, to succeed in this area of our lives. Remember, honesty with yourself opens the door to success. Practice will bring success and prosperity into your life. Again, I say that there is no mistake, because it is a universal law and it cannot be changed by anyone at anytime for any reason. We know that God Himself wouldn't go back on His word. He wouldn't ever change His word for any reason whatsoever; for we know that God's word lasts forever. Amen.

Think loving and kind thoughts about others, show others that you really do care, and that you have love inside of you that you are willing to share with others and with the world around you, and the rest will take care of itself. It is very easy to do. All it takes is a happy smile, a loving and kind smile, and, if need be, practice at making that smile a reality in your life. The more you practice your smile, the better life seems to get. It is a promise that cannot be broken by anyone. It is reality in our lives; it is happiness in life. Learn to smile like a child, as Jesus said, and you will find joy and happiness in your life, for yourself and for others around you.

Smiling at someone else is not hard to do, so let's just do it and make it a habit. You will see how rewarding it can be when you see other people smiling at you all the time, simply because they like your loving smile and want to share the same loving smile with you.

But, remember: be perfectly honest with this practice, with yourself and with others. Sometimes we have to work on it, and that also requires discipline and practice, but it is very rewarding.

Remember that we cannot fool the world, because it only works with true love and happiness, and not just with a made-up appearance. We would only be fooling ourselves and no one else, so don't let that happen. Be truthful with yourself and others.

When we try to fool someone else, we are not getting anywhere. We are at a standstill, unable to succeed and prosper, because we are too busy fooling ourselves while trying to fool others. It just doesn't work; forget it.

So, people who try such half measures are just backsliders in life, people who keep wondering why nothing seems to go right in their lives, no matter what they do or how hard they try.

I said it before and I'll say it again: unless you deal with the truth, face to face, you just won't get anywhere in life. I am talking about physical and spiritual life, whether it is visible or invisible, whether it fits our liking, or whether we find it easy to do. It is something that just must be done, and it has to be done by everyone. There are no excuses and no mistakes, for it is God's law. Amen.

Our brother, Jesus Christ, came on this earth, mainly to teach the truth about the reality of life to everyone. Two thousand years later, here we are with so many people who are still blind and living in spiritual darkness.

Jesus, in the book of Matthew, He taught the world the truth about the physical life. He also taught the truth about the spiritual life, with His death on the cross and His resurrection afterward. He suffered to death on the cross so that we could see and understand the meaning of His teaching, about the reality of life and the truth about life itself. On the third day of His death,

He came back and proved to the world that His teaching was the truth, and nothing but the truth. I believe that the message was strong enough, don't you?

Our brother, Jesus, suffered to death, because He loved us as His brothers, and He wanted us to know that His teaching was true. He wanted us to understand the truth about the reality of life, physically and spiritually. After all that He did, why is the world still living in spiritual darkness?

Why is there so much hatred and suffering in the world today? It is not getting any better; in fact, I believe that it is getting worse. You will understand why, and what could be done about it, after you finish reading and studying this book.

The teaching of Jesus was all about the truth, humanity, and the universe and all that it contains, for our own use and for our own benefit. But to understand it and to profit from it, we must be willing to *listen and obey*. However, for some strange reason, it seems as if people think that they are smart enough, that they don't have to listen to anyone if they don't want to listen, and still everything should be all right with them. Well, I believe that is called stubbornness. I think that everyone knows that there is nothing loving about this disease, and sometimes stubbornness will keep us stuck in a bad rut. As long as we refuse to change, refuse to give up our evil stubbornness, refuse to be honest, face the truth, and deal with it with honestly, then unfortunately, we must stay behind and persist in struggling in life.

But, it doesn't have to be that way. Just because we become adults doesn't mean that we shouldn't listen to others any longer. If we want things to go the proper way in our lives, then we must stop for a moment and think hard. We must make a decision, a good decision, and that decision should be to take a good look at ourselves. We also must be willing to change whatever needs to be changed, even though change seems so difficult to do sometimes. Our own stubbornness may keep us stuck in a bad rut for so long in our lives, until we decide to do something about it. We must be honest with ourselves and be willing to deal with the truth, face to face, never back down, and keep pressing on until we see good results coming from our efforts.

Being stubborn, when it comes to changing something we must change within ourselves, doesn't hurt anyone else but ourselves. Stubbornness will keep us down as long as we let it interfere.

Sometimes, refusal to take a good look at ourselves could be only because we might be afraid to see what we don't want to see. We might be afraid to deal with the truth face to face. Sometimes, our refusal could be because of past events that we don't want to revisit. It could be something that was hard to handle before, and so we don't want to experience it again. That's very understandable, but even so, it is still there inside of us if it wasn't dealt with properly before, and in some cases, it could haunt us all our lives if we don't get rid of it.

Therefore, if past events are unresolved, we should get rid of the unfortunate events by following the few steps you are about to go through in your reading. Whether you approve of it, I am leaving it up to you. I only ask you to please make an effort in understanding. It is far too important to leave it or to just ignore it. Understanding the purpose is for your own benefit.

In any case, I strongly suggest that you leave the past behind you. However, before you can do that, you must take certain steps. If you have offended someone in any way, if possible, make it right with this person. This will allow you to be forgiven by this person, so that you can feel free enough to forgive yourself, too. However, if it is not possible to make it right with this person, then, if you have a sincere heart, and you are willing and ready to repent for what you've done, God will forgive you your trespasses.

Now, just stop, relax, and forgive yourself for whatever you need to forgive yourself for, and ask God to forgive you also. Believe that He has already forgiven you, for God forgives those who forgive themselves, and that means all of us, or any of us, anytime, anywhere. We know that our heavenly Father can do much greater things then we could ever do; therefore, if you can forgive yourself and forgive anyone that ever offended you, then you can be certain that God has already forgiven you. But remember: if you want to live in harmony and peace, then you must repent with a sincere heart and forgive yourself. Once you can forgive yourself, then you know that God has forgiven you also. Then and only then can you leave the past behind and go on living with piece of mind and harmony, with the rest of society forever, with joy and happiness in your heart.

When you live with piece of mind, it is easy to deal with the truth face to face and to be truly honest with yourself and others. When you can live that kind of life, then you can get some understanding about the truth of the reality of life, as Jesus taught us.

Once you get some understanding about the reality of life, you find that life is much easier to handle. You find that there is happiness, true happiness for you also, and you can live a very joyful life. That is God's plan for all of us: to live a peaceful, happy, and joyful life in harmony with everyone.

Let us now take a moment to relax and think about what we've read so far.

I believe that it is more profitable for anyone to stop reading after a few pages, concentrate on what was read, and try to grasp the proper understanding of it before proceeding to the next pages.

There is no point in proceeding any farther, if you don't have the proper understanding of what you have already read. I would suggest that you go back to the beginning of the chapter. Please read it, and study it again properly.

Please stop now.

While you are reading the contents of this book, you may wonder from time to time if you should accept and agree with the messages this book brings to you.

I leave it entirely up to you to make your own decision, but I must tell you that, if you have any difficulties understanding the messages of this book, or agreeing with them, then I strongly suggest that you take your own Bible and check it yourself as you read this book.

Myself, I would prefer that you do it this way, because I know that it would make it easier for you to grasp the proper understanding about the reality of life. You will soon realize that what this book contains is the truth, and nothing but the truth, and you can put your entire trust in what these messages reveal to you.

I say to you that without the power of love, this book wouldn't have been written. Put your mind at ease, read on, accept the true meaning about the reality of life, and grasp the proper understanding of all that this book offers you.

My heart is with you as you learn from these words, and may

God bless you with your study so that you can have the proper understanding.

I know that after reading and studying this book, along with your Bible, you will feel happier, stronger, and blessed.

We now know that anyone who wants to find happiness, success, and prosperity in life first must be honest with himself. Next, one must work hard mentally to develop the proper understanding of the reality of life and to become intelligent enough to know what physical and spiritual life really is.

We know that everyone should know and understand more about spirituality, but before we can even start understanding spirituality, we must know and understand the physical part of life. We need to understand what the reality of life really is, and its purpose, and live in accordance with its purpose, before we can attempt to walk on the spiritual path.

We can be determined to succeed in our lives, but we must know what step to take first and then press on.

We must study, listen, and obey, and with this practice, we must do lots of integrated thinking to get to the proper understanding about physical and spiritual life. Once we get to the proper understanding, then we have to put it into practice. As I've said before, the more we practice, the better and easier it gets.

Remember that with honesty and true love, we can't fail, because love never fails. By putting these tools into action in our lives, we can't help but succeed and prosper in all areas of our lives.

We also must remember that we need some dedication, willingness, courage, and discipline, thought, and control (D.T.C.) to achieve our goals in life.

It may sound like a lot of work, or it may seem as if it is very hard to do, but it is really not so hard; it only seems that way. Once we start working on it, and we start feeling things changing for the better in our lives and inside of us, then we can start feeling the reward that awaits us. That's when we can start feeling proud of ourselves, for letting God into our lives and letting him help us. We can also start having the true faith in ourselves that we should have in reality.

When we start having those feelings, we find it much easier, and we develop more courage and strength to keep pressing on. As we keep pressing on, it becomes easier and easier, and happiness comes in. The happier we get, the more we want to keep pressing on. We don't even want to look back, because we gain in intelligence and wisdom, and experience happy feelings inside of us. Happiness is probably the best feeling that you ever had, but it is just the beginning. It is a true feeling, and it is certainly a feeling to be happy with and proud to have.

When we practice this kind of living and have that happy, proud feeling, then everyone else sees it and feels the goodness in us. They can feel the power of love flowing from us, and everyone feels attracted to and loves us. People want to be our friend forever, because it feels good to be with us. People experience the feelings of love, kindness, joy, happiness, and so forth that emanate from us.

A person who lives this way and feels this joy of life can't help but become successful. I don't think that anyone who has found this new life would want to look back, because the new life is so much better than the old one.

I've seen people who were afraid to look back. I knew someone who said that he didn't want to look back because the old life was far too ugly and facing it was scary. He didn't even want to think about the past, only the future, because there are much better things to look forward to in the future then he had experienced in the past. I could share these same scary feelings and experiences about myself with anyone else, too.

Many of us could and should share these kinds of feelings and experiences with someone else, but human weakness prevents us from doing so. Shyness or fear that someone else might laugh at us may prevent us from sharing. Perhaps we just don't want to bother anyone else with our problems. It might simply be that we don't feel like it, because we are tired of talking about it and about ourselves.

But, it shouldn't be that way, because sharing your feelings and experiences with someone else can be a great help to yourself, and it can also be a great help to the person with whom you are sharing it. Without even knowing about any benefits, this person would be thankful because you've shared something with them, something that may have been very valuable to them, whether it was sharing your problems or your good fortunes. It may have been a great help to them because it was just what they needed to hear, what they were waiting for so that they could work on solving their problems, too. They would be very thankful for what you've done in helping them, and that help happened just by your being willing to share different things with someone, anyone.

Don't be afraid. Don't hesitate to share your problems or your good fortunes with anyone. We are all brothers and sisters, so we should share with each other and help each other. In reality, we also know that it is God's will for all of us to share this way, because then we are living in harmony with each other, and therefore, we are living in harmony with all humanity, the universe, and all the creations that are there for all of us to benefit from equally.

Therefore, it is a universal law that is being ignored by too many people all over the world, and because of that, instead of solving problems in our lives and in the entire world, the problems just keeps getting worse. More problems keep coming into existence all over the world, which makes it more and more difficult for humanity to live in harmony and happiness, as God intended our life to be lived. Human weakness is usually the cause of our problems and for bringing more problems into existence in our world.

Human weakness includes many things. It can mean self-righteousness or selfishness. Sometimes it is valuable to feel good about ourselves, for doing beneficial things for ourselves or someone else. However, it is never good to be selfish, because selfishness is an evil disease that can't and shouldn't be tolerated by anyone at anytime, anywhere in this universe. Such an evil disease causes many problems, including sickness and poverty; it destroys happiness and even causes death.

We exercise wisdom when we refuse to tolerate such evil disease in our lives. Wise people will recognize the disease and how destructive it could be; therefore, they don't allow it in their lives. They reject it; they don't need it, and they don't want it. Therefore, they will not allow it do any damage in their lives. These people use discipline, thought, and control (D.T.C.).

These wise people are usually the happy people that we often see on the street or at our reunions, usually with a smile on their face. We can easily detect that it is a true smile, a smile from being happy with themselves, their loved ones, and even happy with their own lives. They are living in harmony with society, because of the way they control their own lives, as life should be controlled, with love and harmony. They have found joy and happiness. These people are living in harmony with society and with the whole universe. They have peace of mind; therefore, they are living a peaceful and happy life.

These wise people reject any evil, and prevent it from entering their homes and their lives. They are happy and successful people who are able to let anyone else see what it is like to live a happy life. Just by their actions, we cannot help but to see the joy in them.

After reading and studying this book, when you can put all the puzzle pieces together, then you will see clearly and you will understand the whole meaning of this concept. You will see the whole picture as it is in the reality of our lives.

You will understand why these people are living in harmony, happiness, and success, as explained earlier. I am convinced that you are already putting some puzzle pieces together and are probably starting to understand where this reading and study is taking you. I am also convinced that you are already feeling better about yourself, because of what you have already learned, and I want you to know that I am feeling happy for you. Just remember that because you've asked God to be with you, and to bless your reading and studies, He is with you and He is helping you. Know that it is because of Him that you have the will and the ability to learn and understand. Feel happy and blessed with this knowledge.

Now I suggest that you stop reading and concentrate on what you have read up to this point. Please make sure that you properly understand what you have read before you proceed into the next chapter. Please stop now.

Review: Chapter 1, Development

As previously mentioned, the first chapter was designed to help anyone begin developing an understanding of the truth about the reality of life, from physical to spiritual.

This chapter has been an eye-opener for some people, offering a new concept about life. In other words, it offers a new and better way of looking on life as it should be seen and understood, viewing both the physical and spiritual, because the real life starts with physical and finishes with spiritual. I hope that this first chapter has been a great help for you to start developing the proper understanding about the reality of life and its purpose. I certainly hope you could put some of the puzzle pieces together by the end of the chapter. I hope the text helped prepare you so that it can be easier to get the proper understanding for the remainder of the book. This section of the book covers a big part of our lives: how life is dealt with and how it should be dealt with.

We know that there is much more information that could be given on the reality of life, but we must digest it and, in some ways, try to make it understandable by anyone who really needs this help or this information. Choosing the most beneficial information is one of the reasons why we always pray to our heavenly Father to help us with our work and our understanding as we develop while going through this book. We wish this book to be inspirational to anyone reading and studying it.

As I mentioned at the beginning, this book wouldn't have

been written without the power of love. Without this love, I wouldn't even have had the urge to write this book. My main reason for writing it was that I wanted to reach out and help anyone I could help in any way I could help him or her. I believe that this book was the best way to convey my message and reach so many people all over the world. The more people I can touch with the teaching of God, the happier I feel about it. I know that this is what God wanted me to do, and this book is the best way I can share my love with as many people as I can.

Therefore, in this first chapter, we've talked about many major points that we have to deal with most every day of our lives.

We have talked about some gifts or abilities, which we call tools. We discussed what they really are, how they work, and how powerful they can be if we use them in the proper manner and at their proper place.

We've also talked about how much joy and happiness sharing can bring to people's lives. But mainly, sharing puts us in harmony with the whole society and the whole universe. Nothing can go wrong as long as we are living in complete harmony with all.

Once you have learned all about these great tools and know how to put them to work for you, then you can't fail. It isn't possible to fail, because it is also God's universe. God's plan includes tools for everyone to use, to succeed and prosper with them. There is no mistaking it. We really have to realize that using these tools is the only way to prosper, and there is no other way; no matter what we do or try, nothing else works. We just keep on falling and struggling, so a little study and effort only helps anyone who is willing to work. It is for one's own benefit and no one else. Once you know all about these great tools and how they work, then just put them into practice, work with them as often as possible, and you will find that, after a while, using them becomes easy, like a habit. Live with it every day with no effort whatsoever, and you are living in harmony. Therefore, you are living in happiness, joy, and prosperity. You have everything anyone could need or want in life with no limitation, because by that time, you have reached peace of mind and soul. Once we've reached that stage in our lives, then we have reached God Himself, who communicates the proper way, the only way.

As mentioned before, enter your closet and close the door behind you. Be there alone with your Father, which is in secret, and there He will hear you. He also will answer you in secret. One of the reasons why I am saying that He will answer you in the secret is simply because, when we communicate with God in secret, we don't go out on the street corners and shout to the world what God told us. It is between you and your God, and no one else. But, that doesn't mean that you can't use that information to help someone else. The idea is no one should boast about the results of the communication with God. The ability or power you may have received from God might just be taken away from you because you've boasted about it. It is not God's will for anyone to do such a thing.

Just think of it this way: if someone tells you something secretly and expects that it should be kept between the two of you, and then you go and tell someone else about it, do you really think that this person will ever trust you with a secret again? I don't believe so, or at least, I wouldn't. So, why should God trust you with secrets if you can't even keep your word with Him?

Realize what it really means to enter our closet, close the door behind us, and be absolutely alone with our Father. We communicate with Him in silence and in secret. All this really means is to go somewhere where you know that you will be absolutely alone, without any disturbance from anyone or any noise of any kind, and there be absolutely quiet, close your mind to the world, and focus only on God. He is there waiting for you to communicate with Him, and that is the best way to communicate with Him and get your answers. One cannot or should not take what was received in the private silence and bring it out to the open and boast about it. Boasting like this is probably one of the worst things anyone could do. I would be afraid to stop or damage my communication with God for the next time that I wanted to meet God in secret again. I would have difficulty facing Him again. It would certainly take lots of repentance on my part before I would even have enough nerve to meet Him again.

When you communicate with God, make it a covenant between you and your God, and keep it that way. Honor Him and you will never have to be afraid to meet Him again or repent for boasting about it. Instead, you will be anxious and very happy to meet Him again with joy, peace of mind and soul, and with an opened heart. You can be certain that He will receive you with open arms, as a loving Father greets a child. There are no mistaking only good solid results. The silence is where our questions are answered, where we receive success, prosperity, harmony, health, wealth, joy, and happiness that last forever. Honesty and persistence really pays off, and once we have that, then our duty is to pray for others so that they too can get the same. Keep it going and help others reach the tremendous reward as we did. The more saved souls there are, the bigger the happy family gets. All will live in perfect harmony with each other, and this is exactly what our heavenly Father really wants from all of us.

In this first chapter, we also talked about how so many people all over the world live in poverty and struggle with sickness and disease through their whole lives. It is so sad to see, and yet it shouldn't be so very hard to change this situation around so they could live a much better life. If only they knew how and had the proper faith and understanding needed to do that.

We know that people all over the world are praying for those who suffer. I am certain that it helps to a certain degree, but I also believe that it would be more beneficial for these people if they learned how to pray to get results from their own prayers. I am certain that there are many preachers, theologians, and so forth that could be of great help in teaching these people how to pray to get answers. I believe that there should be school classes to teach and practice on this subject, since it is such important matter in everyone's life. Learning about prayer would be beneficial for everyone.

We also spoke about the power that there is in believing without seeing, which means having faith in God that things will happen if we simply believe. As stated in this chapter, "do it, believe it, and let it happen," without any doubt whatsoever, and consider it done. For without the slightest doubt, your faith has made it happen.

But, we also talked about one of the biggest problems that we encounter in our lives is the fact that we lack faith in ourselves and in our heavenly Father. We may think that we have enough faith to make things happen, but we really don't understand what real and true faith really is. Unfortunately, we remain living in darkness or blindness of the truth of it all.

We also talked about how difficult it must be for our heavenly Father to see us struggle through our lives, while it is not necessary for us to do so. But there isn't anything He can do to help us, unless we simply call on Him to help us with our problems. We know that if we don't call upon Him to help us, He can't do anything about it. It is all up to us to decide for ourselves, because He gave us this right. It is for us to use this right in the proper way and for the proper reasons. As I've said before, God doesn't leave us behind. We are the ones who leave Him behind, usually until we get ourselves in deep trouble and at the bottom of the barrel again. When we're in trouble, we think of Him again, and call upon Him to reach out and help us out one more time. It is so amazing that He never forgets any of us and is always ready and willing to help anyone who calls on Him for help. I suppose it is what we call amazing grace. The grace of the Lord be with you forever. Amen.

I wonder sometimes if God is amazed or surprised with us, since we are so smart that we can even create something ourselves. For example, we can even create our own problems. I really don't think for a minute that God is very pleased with this one, but at the same time, we might have thought God needed something new. If there aren't any problems in heaven, then He certainly had the opportunity to learn all about problems here on earth, whether He wished to or not. We are always creating all kinds of negatives that God wouldn't even want us to have or to deal with, because there is absolutely no time for nonsense like that in life. We don't have any time to waste, and our heavenly Father doesn't have any time to waste, either. So, why do we waste our time with such things instead of just following God's plans to make our lives better and easier? We know that He is always here with us, ready and willing to help us at anytime that we are willing to ask Him to help with any difficulties that we may encounter.

This universe that we live in is for all of us to benefit from, if only we learn how to deal with it or how to live with it. We can profit from all that it has for us to use and live with, because everything that was created in it is good for all of us to enjoy in harmony with the whole society. We all can enjoy and benefit from it all equally, and this is another great blessing from God. We have to understand that He didn't create all that He created just for Himself; it was done just for all of us. He saw that it was good, and He was pleased with it. Genesis 1: 25. We also should be happy and very pleased with it, and we certainly should know how to deal with all of it.

We also talked about all the great gifts and abilities that we've received freely from God, but yet it seems that people have such difficulties using these great gifts and abilities with anyone else. We definitely need to do something about it, while we still have time.

There was also some talk about how people should live their lives, and how we would like them to live their lives. We can't or shouldn't even attempt to force other people to live their lives the way we would prefer it, just because we think that our way is the best way. Nevertheless, we certainly can give good advice. A very good way, and probably the best way, is to teach someone else by our own actions. After all, actions speak louder than words; therefore, it should be a teaching for us also. Instead of attempting to force others to live their lives our way, just because we think we know better, even if we sometimes do, we can't forget that a loving smile and kind words can be a big help in reaching out to help someone else who needs our help. People will turn to us and want to be our friends forever because of the loving kindness that they felt and received from us while having a conversation with them. This is really Christian work, and we have to remember that love is the greatest gift of all. Sharing love with anyone else is the most powerful work that anyone can do or share, and it is certainly very rewarding. The more often we do this kind of work, the more reward we get. The reward that I love to get is the fact that it really makes me happy to see someone else happy. It makes me feel good and happy about myself for making other people feel good and happy about themselves. Therefore, in this way, we both get rewarded for our good work or our good deeds.

We talked about Jesus' teaching, how truthful His teaching was, and how powerful it really was. No other teaching done could ever match the teaching of Jesus; no other teaching has ever been as truthful or powerful. It is the simple reason why His teaching is still the most powerful teaching in the whole world, and always will be, because it is the teaching that touches people the most of all teachings. Therefore, we really should listen, learn, and obey if we really want to get anywhere in our lives.

We also talked about how a person can forget about ugly past events, how we can really forgive others, and also how we can really forgive ourselves. We also talked about being forgiven by God and then living freely with peace of mind and soul, and with an opened heart. We can feel God's blessings coming to us in full measure.

Sharing with others is one of the most wonderful things that we can do. Whether we share good fortunes or problems, it doesn't matter, because sharing is always worth doing. Normally, it doesn't matter with whom we share, because if we share with someone else, then it will help in some ways. It is a universal law, and nothing ever goes wrong by obeying a universal law.

Another topic that we touched up is selfishness, which in my view is one of the most evil diseases, if not the most evil, because we know how much harm it can do too many or to everyone. It destroys happiness, causes illness and fatigue, destroys families, and even kills. Anyone who is wise enough will recognize this evil thing and will be ready to reject it before it can do damage. Usually, these wise people do recognize any of those evil things before they get to them, and they will not allow them to enter their homes. They are smart enough to know what they can do, and they won't even allow evil the chance to enter into their house and family.

Chapter 2
D.T.C.

D.T.C. stands for discipline, thought, and control. Let's start with *discipline*. It is very important to know the real meaning of the word discipline. We must realize how much power there is in the field or from the roots of discipline, because where disciplinary actions are taken, success and prosperity usually result.

Discipline is a word many people seem to be scared of, or don't like, just because they equate the word discipline with punishment, and who likes punishment?

People don't want to face punishment, whether they did right or wrong; therefore, for some people, discipline is a scary word, and they want to avoid it.

But, in my view, discipline means something totally different. Discipline means your way to success, by love, willingness, practice, correction, strength, sacrifices to discover new abilities, new knowledge, developing wisdom, and so on. For example, recognizing our faults and correcting them is an exercise of discipline. Keeping that in mind as often as we can, so that we don't keep making the same mistakes again and again, and just practicing that process as often as we can, requires discipline. This view is certainly not a punishment, as many people see discipline.

If everyone were to use discipline every time it should be applied, then I don't believe that there would be room for any punishment at all, and certainly not for doing wrong. With the proper discipline, for the right purpose, and at the right time, there wouldn't be any wrongdoing to begin with.

Discipline isn't just for someone who already has done wrong; it is also for anyone to use in preventing wrong. In other words, discipline is being prepared and preventing the wrongdoing before it happens. Discipline is a very powerful tool to use if we want to succeed in our lives. Success in our lives doesn't only mean financially, but most importantly, with our health, mentally, physically, emotionally, and spiritually.

It takes honesty and strength for us to use disciplinary actions to better ourselves, to make our life joyful. We must be dedicated and determined enough to make the difference, by making sacrifices to change ourselves to become better people, for ourselves and for the world around us. Whether we are working to change some bad habits for some good ones or just practicing and getting used to doing better things, doing something worth doing requires the exercise of discipline. Thinking good about everyone, for example or smiling as often as possible are ways to create new habits. A true smile on someone's face is a very good sign that there is happiness inside this person. As Jesus said, learn to smile like a child. Everyone should smile, even though it might require discipline and practice. But, it pays off. We are rewarded for those efforts, and in the end, the payoff is well worth the effort.

People all over the world use disciplinary actions to reach their goals. They keep on practicing and pressing on, and never give up until they reach their goal. This dedicated effort is the only way people prosper and succeed in reaching their goals in life.

Another good example is setting aside some time every day to concentrate on God and His laws, or universal laws, as you wish. Try to practice remembering laws during the day, whenever you have the chance. Keep it in mind as much as you can and practice that, instead of wasting your time thinking about things of no value. This kind of disciplinary action to better oneself is useful, because as we know, there is always a reward afterward. Therefore, discipline of this type is certainly not a punishment; it is a very helpful tool, a tool to use in working our way to success, prosperity, and happiness.

Discipline is something that we all need to use in our lives, but not everyone is willing to admit that they need to use this tool. It is one of the best tools people can use to better themselves to succeed and prosper in life, but it takes honesty and D.T.C. to prevail.

Problems cannot be solved unless we recognize them first and deal with them directly with an open heart and mind. We must be ready and willing to accept the responsibility and do whatever is necessary to eliminate the problem and make sure that it never returns. You don't need it, you don't want it, and you don't have to have it, so get rid of it.

Unless you have used discipline to prevent the problem from coming into existence in your life, then it takes disciplinary actions to eliminate problem and keep it out of your life forever. It takes dedication, determination, and practice. I'll be the first one to tell you that it certainly pays off.

It may seem like hard work to some people, but I have to say this: if it does seem too difficult for some people to do, then it is because these people don't have enough faith in themselves. This means that these people have more work to do than others do, and they will need more practice than others need to succeed in those areas.

First, they will have to stop and take a good look at themselves. To succeed in changing, they must recognize who they really are, recognize the problem, and then be willing to take disciplinary actions on themselves to change whatever needs to be changed for the better. Sometimes the most difficult thing to do is to recognize a problem in ourselves and admit it to ourselves that we do have a problem, and become ready and willing to take disciplinary actions to better ourselves. All this means working on some areas of our lives and making some changes for ourselves. The result is that we can live a better and happier life, in harmony with the whole world around us, and live according to God's laws.

Another example is *gluttony*. I don't mean to be harsh, but I have to be truthful. We must be truthful with ourselves and to everyone else also. The real truth is that gluttony is a very big problem in our society today, with a very large percentage of the population. We all have something to do about it, because the ones who have this problem need to use disciplinary actions to get rid of it, and the ones who don't have to deal with the problem probably have already used disciplinary actions on themselves in the past. The discipline paid off because they no longer have this problem or they prevented it from coming into existence in their lives before it could occur.

Therefore, whether we like to admit it or not, and it has to be dealt with sooner or later, and the sooner the better, we know that gluttony is a sin, and we know that gluttony harms people. Gluttony can destroy a person's health. It can make a person suffer, and sometimes even suffer an entire lifetime and cause death. This means that gluttony can make a person suffer to death, if an afflicted person takes no disciplinary actions to get rid of it before it is too late.

We know that some people believe that they cannot help it, or that they are sick, and that nothing can be done about it and so on. Some people really think that way.

Lots of people use that line as an escape from the truth, as a way to avoid facing the fact that they would have to do something about it, which means taking disciplinary actions on themselves. These people would rather not even think about changing, because they don't feel that they could handle it. Perhaps they think they would be ill if they cut down on their eating habit, or whatever else gluttony means to them. They truly believe that they would suffer, and the truth is that, in many cases, some people think that using disciplinary action on themselves to lose weight, if excess eating is the case, is punishing themselves for being overweight. People don't like to be punished for something that they don't believe is their fault, but at the same time, they are missing the point. They don't understand that it is only for their own benefit, and not for anyone else's. Whatever the case, anything can be done if a person is willing. Willingness is the first part, and with faith in oneself and in God to help, anything can be done. You must believe in yourself, and also believe that God is always by your side, willing and ready to help anyone who asks for His help. If you have difficulty believing enough, you must use discipline and practice. I also suggest that you study your Bible, as I've mentioned earlier, along with this book, and don't ever give up. I know that with a bit of effort, you will come to understand and you will achieve your goal, and after a while, you will realize that it wasn't so difficult after all. It only takes honesty, faith in yourself, dedication, and the will to change.

It doesn't have to be so difficult. Anyone can get out of that suffering and learn how to live a happy and healthy life. But you must be honest with yourself, be ready and willing to accept the responsibility and do whatever is necessary to better yourself. It requires work to be done on oneself; it takes D.T.C.

Let me put it this way: you must stop, take a good look at yourself, recognize the faults or the problem, admit to yourself that you do have this problem, plan to do something about it as soon as possible, and decide that right now is a good time to start your disciplinary action. Think about it, plan it, start working on it, and keep practicing it. Before you know it, you will feel better about yourself, you will feel healthier, you will feel stronger, and that's when you will start having the proper control of your life. Then you are on your way to success. You will feel glorified with yourself and with what is really happening inside of you. You will experience a happy feeling about yourself and about life itself.

Again, I say, take it one step at a time: recognize the problem, make a plan to get rid of it, make sure that it is a good plan that will work for you, stick to your plan, and conquer the problem. Finally, rejoice for your success in your plan, and then, when you're ready, go on to the next target. Again, make your plan, conquer it also, and rejoice for your success again, and so on. We can't expect to do it all in one day, so take it slow, one thing at a time, and one step at a time. But, as I've said earlier, with disciplinary actions, you can't help but succeed in different areas of your life. Remember that the more negative a problem you conquer, the more you find success, prosperity, and happiness in your life.

There is such a great reward afterward, that no one wants to look back. You simply persist as it keeps getting better and better, and you keep getting stronger and stronger as you keep working on it. Continue to study, because it will get better and easier for you, and before you know it, you really enjoy working on disciplinary actions, because taking control really makes you happier.

After recognizing what discipline really is and how it works, and using this tool and a while benefiting from it, then you start to enjoy working with this tool. You realize how rewarding it really is, and you find it a very pleasant tool to use.

Now I suggest you stop reading for a while, and concentrate on what you've read until now. Please make sure that you properly understand what you've read before you read any further.

Please stop reading now.

Thought is also one of the key points that we really have to work with; it is a component of D.T.C. It doesn't seem to mean much for many people, but let me tell you that it is no joking matter. Thought is power and reality in our lives.

As some people would say, it is easy to think about anything. However, thinking about anything is one thing, and seriously thinking about true thoughts, good and loving thoughts, positive, true, and happy thoughts about oneself and the rest of society, all humanity and the universe that we live in and God and His laws, is something totally different.

We have heard the old saying: take care of yourself and never mind anybody else. Well, this statement couldn't be further from the truth. This kind of statement would interfere with someone's positive thinking about the reality of life. Sadly, some people think of it as just a joke, without realizing that they are doing wrong. They fail to see how damaging they can be to someone else, just by not thinking properly about what they are about to say before they say it.

No one knows what someone else is thinking at anytime; therefore, no one knows if the next person is thinking about something wrong or bad, or if he or she is thinking good and positive thoughts. Consequently, the person doing much of the talking could be interfering with someone else's positive thinking, without even realizing it.

I am not saying that it is not good to joke around with other people sometimes, but there is a time for joking and there is a time to be serious about what we say. We should think about it and speak what is proper to speak about, and at the proper time and place. We should not just say whatever we feel like saying at anytime anywhere, to just anyone, because if we act in this manner, we certainly have not tamed our tongue. Remember, a wise person is someone who can tame his or her tongue, as we all know that it is one of Jesus' great teachings.

Therefore, if we would think about whatever we are about to say before saying it, many times, we wouldn't even say anything. The result would be that fewer people would get offended, but again, it takes some proper thinking, disciplinary actions, and good control on one's part, or D.T.C.

Our brother, Jesus, said, in anything you do, do it in the glory of God, meaning Our Father, which is in heaven. 1 Corinthians 10, 31. Well, we know that He meant doing good deeds to others, physically and mentally, in our thinking for example. Think good thoughts for everyone, and you will be rewarded openly by God

Our Father. That is a promise that cannot be changed or broken by anyone.

Thinking sincere, kind, and loving thoughts about everyone and all creations is like planting a good seed in a very good and rich soil and watching it grow beautifully.

It could also be the other way around with a bad thought; like a bad seed, nothing good ever comes out of bad thoughts. Likewise, no good fruit comes from a bad seed. It is reality of life; it is a universal law, and it cannot be changed. When a person strives to reach a goal, this person must do some proper planning. It requires some good integrated thinking to make a proper plan to reach that goal. For some people, to reach their goal means more to them than anything else; for them, there is no time for foolish thinking, only time for good integrated thinking. In the end, they get the reward that they well deserve. If you take time to study other people and their actions, you will soon learn that planning is exactly what they have done and they did reach their goal.

Now let me explain something to you, my way, and see whether you can grasp the understanding of it all and see how you would deal with it.

You can use that as a study or practice; it is all in a learning process, and you will gain from it.

Now, I think a kind thought. I think that if I go and visit some friends, and help them for a while with their work, with a smile, and show that I am happy to be able to help them, I think that they will be happy. Or maybe I'll just visit and talk to an old friend, and share happiness and laughter with this person to make him or her very happy.

These are very good thoughts. So now, make a plan: plan a

time and date to go and do what you've thought of doing, and carry on with your plan. Go and do it. Be determined, and don't change your mind an hour later. Don't let anything get in the way and delay you or even stop you. Go ahead and do it, not six months from now or a month or a week from now, do it today or tomorrow, the sooner the better for everyone. Hear this: if you leave home with the thought and desire of making someone else happy, and you are determined to carry on with your plan, and accomplish your task well, I can tell you that by the time that you get back home, you will probably have already received one of the biggest rewards you could ever have received. The reward is, first of all, being happy, happy about what you have done, and you will be proud of yourself for what you have accomplished for someone else. You have all the right in the world to be happy and to be proud of yourself for letting God work with you, and for keeping Him in mind at all times. This is when you start feeling stronger, because when you feel happy with yourself because of your good deeds, that's when you feel yourself getting stronger, and that's when you start having control of your life the way that you should. You will know that someone else is very happy with you, happy to have you as a good and loving friend; with this kind of recognition and happiness, you just can't fail in life. After a while, you have so many people on your side, you have so many people who think good thoughts about you, and it is all because, first of all, you had good thoughts about them. Therefore, you have many people who love you, and we all know that love never fails.

Think a good thought about me and I will think a good thought about you also.

Let me put it to you this way: in a loving family, if someone thinks good thoughts about someone else in the same family, the person that he or she thought of will feel it. For some reason, this person will feel happy, because he or she knows that there is something good and positive happening in the family. This person will sense a good and positive feeling and influence in this family, and that makes this person feel good and happy, to be part of this family. Sometimes they don't even realize why they are happy to be with each other, why they love each other as they do, as brothers and sisters, until they start sharing their thoughts with each other. That's when they realize why they are so close to each other: because they make each other feel good and happy, by their good and positive thinking about one another.

Therefore, since we all know that we are all in the same family of brothers and sisters, and we also know that we are all in the same family of God, I believe that when we pay close attention to our conscience and use some common sense, we can detect either bad feelings or good feelings among the people around us, or even among the whole human race, all over the world. We feel it when there is bad or good influence, good or bad feelings that happen in society anywhere; we feel it.

Think just for a moment about the wars. What brings the wars to action? Bad thoughts do; bad thoughts about someone else, about another leader, or about another country. That gets to the point that the feelings are not very good among some people. Bad influence, disregard and disrespect for each other, and somehow, people finally find a way to make themselves believe that negative thinking or negative actions toward someone else is a good thing to do, and so on.

We have to realize that, because of all those bad thoughts, the whole world feels the impact of wars, hatred, wickedness, and so on.

Some leaders will do some very hard thinking, but it is not always for the good of the nation. It is too often because of their own selfishness, their own wicked thoughts of revenge, or getting even, or just because they want to prove that they are better or smarter then the next one. They don't even think about the real problems, about all the chaos and confusion that they cause for the entire world to see and feel, but nevertheless, whatever they think is what they keep on thinking.

Therefore, those thoughts are certainly not always right, but still they are thoughts, and the whole world feels and sometimes we even suffer for those thoughts, don't we?

There are other, much better thoughts. For example, some people always think of helping others; they reach out to do whatever they can to do good for someone else who is in need of their help. They do it with joy, they are happy to be able to help, and they wouldn't think of anything else but to help in any way they can. Because of their right thinking, they know that their help is needed. They only think of helping, sometime in prayers, sometimes with food or money or clothing, but their thoughts are right. These people certainly have big hearts, and we know that these people will have the reward that they deserve, may God bless them.

Therefore, as I've said before, think a good thought about me, and I will think a good thought about you, too.

Sometimes, when there is a disaster in a certain family, someone else, a friend, will send a letter or even make a telephone call. The friend will say, "Our thoughts are with you," meaning that loved ones are thinking good and positive about those who are suffering. These thoughts are supposed to help the others with their emotional feelings, and friend, believe it or not, it is true. These supportive thoughts do help. There is great power in people's minds with their thinking.

The most powerful and important thing for us in our lives is the way we think and what we think about, especially when we think about someone else. Thinking positively about anyone, or anything at all in the whole universe, is very powerful. The thought of a person is what makes this person a good or a bad person. Think good and positive thoughts all the time, and you will go to heaven; think bad and negative thoughts all the time, and you will go to hell.

Our Bible tells us, do good to others as you want them to do good for you; think good about others if you want them to think good about you. Matthew 7:12. We all know that this is not something I made up on my own, or something I am saying to scare you, or because I am trying to tell you how to live your own life. It is God's law; it is reality and a universal law that cannot be changed or broken by anyone at anytime.

When someone says such things as: relax, breathe easy, go with peace of mind, my thoughts are with you always, these things are a very powerful thing to say to anyone. It is a very strong support to someone else, because it means *I will be with you all of the time, in thoughts,* or *I will always be by your side when you need me, in thoughts,* or *think of me and send me a letter or call me on the phone.* This person knows very well that this is a very strong support through positive thinking for or about one another. It is love, it is reality of life, and it is God's universal law.

As little as we realize it, these kind of thoughts, or this kind of thinking, can heal someone else or perhaps even save someone else's life, without understanding how this could be or how that could happen.

I say to you, if you do understand it, it is very well for you if you act this way, truthfully with someone else. But if you don't understand how it works, don't worry about it; just practice it all the time, and after a while, check it out for yourself. See for yourself how wonderfully it really works and you will feel the great power that is in it. Then you will get to understand it. As I've said, if you don't understand it, don't worry about it; just think good and positive thoughts about all the universe and all that is in it, and good rewards will surely come to you for your good and positive thinking. It is powerful, and it works like magic. After a while, you will get to understand it, because you will get to remember whatever you thought about before the fact, and you probably will realize that your good thought may have made it happen. The next time, you will be anxious to see the result from your good thinking, and then you will know how powerful it really is. You will experience it, and you will see for yourself how it really works like magic, and without a doubt, you will do more work on this good thinking, and you will tell others about it, too.

We also have to realize that a good positive thought about everyone will bring the power of love into action in our lives.

Love of the spirit. As the song says: think of me when you're lonely, think of me when you're blue, think of me when you're far away, and I'll be thinking of you. A great song called "Think of me" (when you're lonely), done by Buck Owens.

This might just be a song, but it does speak the truth, probably more than people realize—maybe even more than the writer of this song realized. But then, maybe the writer understood it and even experienced it sometime in his or her life, and so spoke the truth in a lovely song.

⌁

Control is another key piece of the puzzle in everyone's life. As we know, without control in our lives, we don't get anywhere. If we do get somewhere and then lose control, then we lose it all at the end. It doesn't matter what we have, if we don't have any control over anything, then we would make a mess out of everything, or as I've said, we lose it all.

The same thing goes for self-control. We need to have absolute control, physically, mentally, and emotionally. First, we must have control of our own thoughts, or if we don't, then I strongly suggest that we start practicing. The sooner we do it, the better it will be.

If we want to reach a goal in our life that is very important to us, then we have to do some proper thinking, make a plan, and mentally control this plan to make it work so that we can reach our goal. This also requires D.T.C.

We need to have control of our thoughts, and sometimes, it takes practice. We need to have the ability to accept, or maybe reject, certain thoughts that may come through our mind sometimes. This is control of the thoughts, or control of whatever goes through the mind at anytime. As we know, thoughts slip through our mind without us wanting those thoughts to begin with, but they do come slipping in anyway. Therefore, we must work on having control. It takes practice, and a good way to practice control is to keep reminding yourself that whenever you do detect a negative thought slipping through your mind, you just have to remember that you have an important project you must think about, right now, and it can't wait. If you don't really have any project planned, then just make one up, anything at all just to get you of that negative thought. After you've practiced that for a while, then in a short time, you realize that you don't receive so many negative thoughts, slipping through your mind anymore as they used to. Let me tell you that it sure does feel good to know that it is getting better and easier, because we all know that sometimes it is a real battle just to keep on thinking good positive thoughts all the time, about everything or everyone. If we don't know what to do about it, or how to control it, then unfortunately, we just have to keep on battling with those unwanted thoughts.

If it is a good thought to benefit ourselves and society, then we should practice to keep thinking these kinds of thoughts or practice to keep thinking these kinds of thoughts more often.

We feel good with these kinds of thoughts, but if there is a thought that comes slipping through our mind that is not a good and positive thought for ourselves and for society, then we should have common sense enough to realize that this isn't good for anyone. We should reject that thought and replace it with a good and positive thought immediately.

Keeping that in mind and practicing that as often as we can, it does get better and easier. That is having control of our thoughts. We know that our life here on Earth is so very short, but it can be a good and happy life if we have control of it. It is up to each of us to take control of our own life, because no one else will or can do it for us.

We also certainly need to have control of our tongue. As it is written in our good book, and as I've mentioned earlier, a wise man is a man who can tame his tongue. In other words, control his tongue, talk about something that is worth talking about, at the right time, at the right place, and to the right people. Otherwise, it would be more profitable that this person didn't say anything at all.

Taming our tongue shouldn't be so very hard to do, because it should be easier for us to keep our mouth shut, than to be the one doing all the talking. But it seems as if talking is a must for some people who think: I must talk, I have to say something, I can't help it, I just have to open my mouth and let something out, as if their tongue wants to speak with or without the person's will or permission. Let me say this the way I see it and as I know it: a wise person is a person who listens and learns. It is much more profitable for anyone to listen and learn than for anyone to do much talking, unless of course, this person is a teacher of the truth. Therefore, while one listens and learns, the other doesn't have the chance to learn anything because he or she is too busy doing the talking. Well, I say that it is lack of control, mentally and physically, and anyone who has this kind of problem controlling their tongue, sooner or later ends up with more problems. As stated in Chapter 1, this person is the creator of his or her own problems, and these problems are created because of lack of control.

Well, we know that we can't or shouldn't even try to control anyone else's life or behavior, but we certainly can help by the way we control our own lives. The better we control our lives, the more helpful it will be to others. Actions speak louder than any words we say, so the best thing to do is less talking and more leading by example.

We must be careful with this concept because if we want our children or someone else to learn from our actions, then we need to make sure that we have proper control of our own lives and that we are capable of showing them the proper way. Some discipline on our own part is also required to make certain that we are doing the right thing. It certainly shouldn't be just to satisfy ourselves or for our own benefit, but specially to benefit others. If so, then we have the perfect right to be happy with ourselves, for what we've done for someone else, and then we can't help but be recognized and rewarded for our good deeds.

Sometimes it is difficult for us to be willing to change our ways, to teach someone else the proper ways. As I've mentioned before, it certainly takes true love and understanding for us to take proper control of our lives and to be willing to change some of our ways to teach someone else the proper way simply because we care that much. This is really taking real control of our life, and if we are that strong, and willing to do that much for anyone else, surely, we can't go wrong in our lives, and success and prosperity will follow.

We have to remember that if we want to teach someone else, we have to make sure that we are doing the right thing or we shouldn't do anything at all. We can play around with our own lives all we want, but when it comes to someone else's life and future, no one has the right to decide what kind of life or future the other should live. And it shouldn't be mistaken by anyone, make no mistake: one person cannot force another person to live his or her life the way this other person wants it lived. It is neither a universal law nor the will of God.

Anyone who tries to control someone else's life just for personal benefit, or just to have their way with them, is just someone who has no control over their own lives, because they are too pre-occupied by trying to control someone else's life. While they think that they have control of everything, they have lost control of their own lives without even realizing it, and that can become very sad, and it can also be harmful to anyone especially themselves.

By using D.T.C. properly, we can't fail. We succeed and prosper in life, with harmony, joy, and happiness.

I say these words, not only because I feel like saying them, but because it is the truth, and it is taught to us all from our Bible. We all know that it is reality in our lives; it is God's teaching because it is His will, that we have control of our own lives and doing what is right for ourselves and for all humanity. It pleases Him and because of that, He rewards us openly. Jeremiah 31:16. Galatians 5:22. which are the fruits of the Spirit.

We know that lots of people have real problems with D.T.C. in their lives, especially when it comes to controlling their thoughts and their tongues. As funny as it may sound, some tongues even seem to speak without their owner even thinking first about what was said. The person realizes what happened, or what was said, only after it was already said. The person wonders how such thing could have happened.

Sometimes when someone makes this sort of mistake, instead of feeling embarrassed or foolish, that person will try to change the story or make a joke out of it. But people know what's going on, and instantly, everyone sees that this person has lost control of his or her tongue. Of course, the person knows that no thought was given before speaking, and this person ends up feeling badly. In fact, the person hurts inside for doing something foolish in front of other people.

Please don't let that happen to you. Think before you talk, and you will not have to worry about making a fool of yourself. Make sure to use common sense and talk sensibly, or you will be better off not to say anything at all.

Sometimes people lose control of their thoughts and tongues, especially when it comes time to talk negatively about someone else who they don't seem to like. They make that negative talk a habit and it goes on and on and, before they know it, they seem to have problems in different areas of their own lives. They get frustrated about it, and they don't seem to understand why they always seem to have those problems coming up in their lives. They don't even know what caused it.

I would like to call that creating a negative influence, and then feeding it with those negative thoughts and words, about or against someone else, every chance they get. But people can get caught up so easily with those bad habits and fail to even realize that they really are the creators of those problems. They also don't realize how so very dangerous those bad habits can become in someone's life. We know that negative influence destroys happiness, and we know that without happiness, there isn't much to look forward to in life. In fact, without happiness, there isn't even much interest in anything.

Therefore, there would be a necessity to use the D.T.C. tools and work with them, and practice with them. Don't lose any time, because the sooner you use them, and the harder you work with them, the better it will be. The sooner you will see results and progress for yourself and for everyone else also, because the sooner you get rid of those bad habits and replace them with good ones, the sooner you will find peace and happiness, especially with yourself and that certainly is the best part.

When someone lets himself or herself get in such situation, and refuses to get out of that terrible situation, it is self-persecution, as Jesus calls it. It is very sad to see that these people are just keeping themselves in persecution, without even realizing it, because unfortunately, they don't understand this reality, and they don't realize how badly damaging it is to their lives.

Some people think that they are happy, just the way they are, with this kind of attitude or bad habit, and they just don't know what they are missing in their life. They won't even try to correct themselves or the problem, because they think that they are fine just the way they are, that there isn't anything wrong. They really are not intelligent enough to see it, and they really don't want to see it, either. Some other people may or may not understand what they are really missing, but the truth is that many times, it is just because they are too lazy to make even the smallest effort to get out of that terrible rut in which they are stuck. This is really lack of control on someone's part. These people usually miss the boat, as we say, and the sad part of it is that these people usually lie to themselves and to others, just to try to make themselves feel better about the whole situation. They really never get anywhere worthwhile, and they just keep on persecuting themselves, because of lack of self control or because they can't overcome their laziness. I urge you to use these D.T.C. tools and work with them. It is really an intelligent thing to do, and these tools will benefit you much more then you think. Please try them for real, and be completely honest about it; after all, it is for your own benefit. I promise that you will find true happiness because you will find real peace of mind.

If you have any problems and difficulties using these tools, don't worry, because God is always with you and always willing and ready to help anyone who asks Him at anytime. So, if you have any problems using these tools, just ask for help and He will be right there to help you. There isn't anything more intelligent for us to do than to speak to God and sincerely ask Him for help, or for whatever else we need from Him.

We talk more about persecution further ahead in this book.

Now again, please stop reading and concentrate on what you've read so far. Make sure that you really understand what you've read before reading any further. Thank you.

Please stop now.

Promise me that you will study this book properly, and I promise you that you will be happy and blessed by the time you finish working through it.

Review: Chapter 2, D.T.C.

We have talked about D.T.C. and starting with discipline. As we know, some people seem to think that discipline is something like a punishment, but it is really the contrary of that. Discipline is a guide or a way to success and prosperity, and we know that everyone needs discipline to get anywhere worthwhile in life. In my view, it means something very great for all of us. Discipline allows us to improve in life, become a better person, and become a smarter person. We can cope with life in a better and easier way, because discipline is something in the line of practice, willingness, correction, strength and sacrifices to discover new abilities, new knowledge, developing wisdom, and so on, but it is certainly not punishment. In fact, I would be willing to say that if people use self-discipline to better themselves, it would be a blessing to them just to do that to upgrade or advance themselves in their lives. I really don't think that just anyone can actually do that much for themselves, and most of the time, it is just because of lack of willingness, or the real truth is laziness, in many cases. But, in any case, everything can be overcome with a bit of effort and some disciplinary action on oneself. Don't ever quit or even think of it, because it is far too important in everyone's life.

D.T.C. also involves thought, which is so very important in our lives, and probably more important than people really think. As we discussed in this chapter, anyone can think about anything; it's very easy. But there is true thinking, for example, thinking good and positive thoughts about someone else, or even about the whole society. You may even think good thoughts about someone who even tried to hurt you or your family. I understand that it can be difficult to do at times, but remember that the harder it is to do, the bigger the reward for doing it. At the same time, you are releasing this person from his trespasses, and at the same time, you are also freeing yourself from the bondage of hanging on to what someone else has done. You don't need the load on your shoulders; therefore, let go of it by forgiving this person, then go on and forget about it. It's not worth it to carry that load with you for the rest of your life. Proper thinking can go a long way, because proper thinking will make you realize that the only way to do it is to release this person, forgive him or her, and you know that you are also released from this nonsense of hatred, grudge, jealousy, or whatever it may be. Set yourself free from all resentments, condemnation, or any other negative that could hold you back from walking on the right path.

Therefore, good thinking always bring good results, the same way that bad thinking will always bring bad results. I really believe that there are too many bad thoughts in society, and if there weren't so much nonsense, then this place would be a much better place to live and enjoy. As I've said before, think good thoughts about me, and I will think good thoughts about you also. It is a fact that if someone thinks good thoughts about you, you feel those thoughts in some ways; but if someone is thinking bad thoughts about you, you also feel them in some ways. Even if you don't take time to think about what is really happening, it is still there and you do feel it. If you don't really believe this statement, then just keep it in mind and try it out sometime. Check it out, and you will realize that you may get startled by it when you realize that it is the absolute truth.

We already know that if we want good results in our lives, then we must have or develop good and positive thoughts all the time. This is the only way that brings people to be happy or to get to know what happiness really is. Once you know the power of having positive thoughts, then make a habit of it and live with it. Make others happy also by showing your own happiness to the world around you, and not just your friends or your loved ones, but to everyone you meet, no matter who it is. This comes from good thinking.

If you really think of it, even if something didn't seem to go very well today, that's not the end of the world. Tomorrow is another day. Try to make it go better, and then the next day, and the next. Just keep thinking positive, and you can be certain that things will turn out right.

Therefore, the very first thing is you must have complete control of your thoughts, and you, yourself, will make things go the proper way for yourself and for others also. You make it happen this way by your own thoughts, because we very well know that what you think or build up in your inner thoughts is what you will produce on the outside. This isn't just my opinion, but it is a very strong teaching from the Bible. Matthew 12:35, Luke 6: 45. It is a universal law, and no one or nothing can change this law. But if anyone doesn't understand what the universal law really is, then let me put it this way as an example. We do understand the law of gravity, and there is absolutely nothing that we can do about it. Air, for example, is another universal law that nothing can be done about, since we cannot think one thing and produce another thing at the same time. That leaves us with the answer that whatever we produce inside our mind is what we will produce on the outside also. That's just the way things are in the universal world, and we have to realize that we are really blessed that it is the way that it is. I for one am very glad that none of that can be changed, because it is perfect just the way it is.

Therefore, remember that when we have complete control of our thoughts, we can be certain that things are going to go the proper way in our life. Remember D.T.C., and work with it every day. You will surely succeed in all areas of your life, and prosperity will follow.

Chapter 3

Intelligence

Intelligence is one of the biggest puzzle pieces in everyone's life. Most of us are born with average intelligence; a very few don't develop intelligence at birth or shortly after, but they do develop intelligence later on in life, and at a slower pace than others do perhaps. And, for a very few, it is unfortunate that they never hardly develop intelligence. But most of us are fortunate enough to start developing intelligence the second we are born or even before birth.

Some of us develop intelligence quicker and younger than others do. Sometimes an adult can make a very important difference with a child's intelligence development in a very young age. Adults should keep a close watch on a child for signs that would lead them to believe that this child is going to be very intelligent, and certainly should be helped in whatever way that would be necessary to help this child grow in the proper way and in the proper speed. However, it cannot be overly done or done too rapidly, or that could be harmful to the child's development.

Don't get me wrong here, because of the way I am putting this into perspective. But what I am saying is that some children develop mental abilities differently than others do, sometimes faster than others do. I believe that their ability should be looked at in a different way and should be worked at in a different way. We know that certain children should be worked with in a different manner than others, according to their mental development and their mental abilities. Anyone who has some common sense shouldn't have any difficulties recognizing or realizing this fact, and should work with the child accordingly. But if a person doesn't know how to work with these children, then help should be obtained from someone else who knows how to work with children the proper way. Proper care will benefit the child. Don't take any chances; get the proper help, and you will be happy that you did afterward.

For example, if a child happens to be a thinker and seems to be creative, then this child is mentally growing, developing intelligence, and this child should be noticed by adults and helped with his or her development. If the adult realizes what is happening with the child, and realizes the great importance, then the adult should do whatever is necessary to help the child with his or her mental development. There should be no time wasted.

Sometimes it is more important than we realize to just stop and listen to what a child has to say and give the child an answer or advice. Many times, a child is looking for support, a helping hand just to sort out his or her thoughts and wonders. Sometimes it doesn't take very much to satisfy a child's need for information or encouragement.

But we have to be very careful with our advice and answers, because a child could grasp some information very quickly. Children don't forget so quickly, and we have to realize that if a child comes to us for an answer or advice, that means that this child has put his or her trust in us. We have to be certain that this trust remains in this child. Trust is one of the most important things for a child, who is able to trust an adult forever.

If a child puts his or her trust in a certain adult, then this person should in all respects make absolutely certain that he or she knows the proper answer or advice to give to this child. Otherwise, it could become disaster for this child's trust for an adult if the child realizes that he or she was mislead with a wrong answer or bad advice by a trusted person.

Such mistakes made by an adult to a child should never happen, because they could be very destructive to a child's mental development. Such mistakes could cause a child to struggle while growing up, just because of the trust that he or she once had and lost, just because of wrong information he or she received in the past. This child finds it so difficult to truly trust anyone again. This child feels alone and sometimes the load is just too heavy for the child to carry. This situation is the farthest thing from what should happen for any children while they are trying so hard to grow up successfully.

So I say, please let's be absolutely certain that we have the proper answer or advice to give to a child before we even think of giving an answer or advice. We certainly don't want to mislead and harm anyone who has trust in us.

Sometimes the problem is that an adult wants to show that he or she knows more than the next person knows and is quick at giving an answer or advice, without realizing how important it is to be really truthful and careful. Truth can make good friends for life, but mistakes can turn people away from you for the rest of your life. I'm sure that no one really wants that result, which is something that is surely not needed in our lives. So I say please, think properly before giving an answer or advice to anyone, and keep the trust growing among us. It is an intelligent thing to do, to make life easier for everyone.

We have to realize that if there is real trust between two persons, then there is happiness with these two persons. If there is happiness, there is also strength and success. They are living in harmony with each other. But that doesn't mean only people that live together in the same home; it can just be truthful friends. Being truthful to everyone is an intelligent thing to do at all time, and this also shows a very good example to others so that they can also learn and practice to live with this kind of attitude. They in turn can also teach others by their actions.

If this kind of behavior can occur with two persons, and develop a great trust among them, then why not take the same actions toward more people, so that more people can also have trust and be happy, and have a better chance in succeeding in reaching their goal in their lives?

Real trust can bring joy and happiness in people's lives. It certainly can also bring success and prosperity, and we have to realize that honesty makes trust a reality for everyone.

Since bringing joy and happiness in someone else's life is a wonderful and a very intelligent thing to do, and it is very rewarding, we should keep that in mind and work on it every chance we get. Watch happiness grow among the people that we share happiness with; it is a joyful thing to see. Try it and see for yourself how good it makes you feel inside.

It makes you feel very intelligent, and you have the right to feel this way, because you deserve it.

It makes me feel joyful just to see someone else acting joyfully. It makes me feel happy just to talk with a happy person. When I to make someone else happy, that also makes me feel happy. I believe that I have the full right to feel this way, and when I feel happy because I've made someone else happy, that makes me feel stronger, and I certainly feel more intelligent.

Remember that an intelligent person is someone who has developed common sense and will only speak the truth. If this person cannot speak the truth, they'd rather not even say a word to anyone about anything.

We know that some people are very successful in their lives, and it is, in part, because they have developed intelligence throughout their youth. Most of the time, it is because they have received help from adults with their mental development while they were young. They continued working on their own, and with their hard work, they developed greater intelligence. With their integrated thinking on their own free will, they got smarter and smarter and became successful in their lives.

Now, we understand that intelligence is a very powerful tool that is being used by many people all over the world. When we have the chance to meet and talk with a successful person, we actually feel the intelligence in that person.

But we have to be very careful about how this powerful tool is being used, because many people are very intelligent, but are not necessarily using this ability in the proper way, or for a good purpose to benefit everyone else.

The proper way to use intelligence should be to benefit ourselves and all society, and not only for ourselves because then we would fall in the trap called selfishness. There is no true prosperity or true success in selfishness, because it can be used in a very evil way. There is no real success or true prosperity in anything evil.

But one can be very successful by using this ability. This powerful tool is helping many people all over the world, because they use it for the right purpose. Then automatically society would make this person successful, because the more we give to humanity, the more we receive in return. One can't help but to receive, it is a universal law that cannot be ignored, or shouldn't be ignored by anyone. It is reality of life, and everyone should know this fact.

But, on the other hand, selfishness is just the tool that would make a person miss the point all together, miss the truth about the reality of life. Therefore, a person could be living in this world yet be separated from the rest of society, because this person would only be looking for his own benefits, and wouldn't really care enough about anyone else.

This is not so very hard to understand. We just have to take a quick look at the governments, political leaders, and bureaucrats who have control over society all over the world.

These political leaders and bureaucrats are very intelligent people, but are more interested in filling their pockets with the hard-working people's money than they are in getting people out of poverty and helping them succeed in their lives. They are keeping people stuck in their claws and won't let go. But I believe that one day will come when they will have no choice but to open their claws, free people, help them get out of poverty, and help people succeed also as it is a universal law that is being sadly ignored by so many people all over the world.

They will have to face the reality of life and deal with the truth face to face, because this is according to God's will, for His people to succeed equally. It will happen, maybe sooner than we think, and the evil trap called selfishness will loosen its grip, and lose the battle. But for now, they all believe that they are very intelligent, but really, they are only intelligent in their own ways.

Because of this selfishness, the world is living in a terrible panic, and fighting and killing each other in the most ugly ways. They are called battles in wars, and these are caused by bad leaders who are supposedly protecting their people from harm.

Other intelligent people in this world are helping others in our society, and they are very successful at what they are doing.

These people are living with an open heart and peace of mind. They have a very good reason to be very happy with themselves, because they know that they are doing what is right. They are doing what is right for society as well as for themselves, because they understand the reality of life and how important it is for everyone to live in harmony, with each other and to succeed equally. How wonderful it would be, just to see the whole human race succeed in happiness.

Anyone who uses his or her intelligence for the benefit of society has a lifelong success. Such a person can't help but be successful, and this person is a very wise person, because he or she uses the tool of intelligence with the power of love, for all humanity. Therefore, this person is rewarded openly, while others are struggling with their own laws and wars, which are all caused by the evil disease called selfishness.

We have to realize that selfishness is a very destructive disease, created not by God, but by man, against God's will.

Now I want you to stop reading for a moment and focus on the success that intelligence can bring in your life, by using it the proper way and for the right purpose, anywhere, anytime with anyone.

Relax. I want you to make sure that you understand the message properly before you read any further.

Please stop now.

Now I hope you have given it good thought and understand what I am getting at before you proceed with the reading. There is no point in proceeding, if you didn't get the proper understanding of what you've already read.

I hope with all my heart that you gave it deep thought and understood, but if you are not sure about it, then I strongly suggest that you go back to the first chapter and read it again. Review is always a wise thing to do in any case, because I believe that any book that contains important information should always be read more than once. The more times you read it, the more beneficial it is for you, because you get the proper understanding to the overall picture.

Like many other books, every word of this book is important. It is somewhat like a puzzle, and as you read it, you have to put the puzzle pieces together to form the picture as you read on. After a while, you start seeing the picture develop. By the end of this text, you will understand what the whole picture represents. Only then will you really understand the true message; only then will you find the answers to your questions.

I bet you're anxious to get to the end, but please take your time reading it, study it properly, and make sure that you understand the whole message properly. Only then will it be helpful to you; only then will you be able to put your feet on the spiritual path. Until then, you have to be patient, and study as you read on.

I hope that you have your Bible by your side at all times, so that you can check things out for yourself, as I have mentioned before. If you have read the Bible before, then you automatically know that there is no mistake concerning the truth about the reality of life in this volume. But if you didn't, then I strongly suggest that you read your Bible, because it is far too important in everyone's life to help us succeed and prosper.

It is my desire to see people succeed and prosper in their lives. What a joy, what rewarding news, it is to know that someone succeeded and prospered in their lives, and what a joy to know that I was able to help someone reach a life goal. What a joy to know that the Holy Spirit is with us and helping us with our understanding.

I, myself, feel that it is one of the greatest, if not the greatest honor, just knowing that God is on our side and helping us all the way to success and prosperity, if only we accept Him and let Him help us, according to His will. As the song says it: "let the Lord have His way, in your life every day, there is no peace, there is no rest, until the Lord has His way, put your life in His hands, rest secure in His plan, let the Lord, let the Lord have His way." This is a very short song, but a very powerful song, that we sing during our Bible studies, every week. I don't know who wrote this song, but we and especially the children really enjoy it.

If you've read the Bible before, then you know what I am talking about and you can understand what this volume is revealing to you. But if you haven't read the Bible, then you need to read it. It is for your own benefit; that is why I am asking you to do so. I know that it will be much more profitable for you, if you check this teaching out for yourself in the Bible.

We know that if you didn't read the Bible before, and you start reading it now, it will take you longer to read and study through this book, but believe me, it will be all for better. You will know this fact after you've been through reading and have studied this book, along with your Bible. I know that you will be very happy that you have followed my instructions, and you will feel blessed with what you have learned through it all.

If you set this as your goal to reach, then you will feel joyful and very strong, because you will have put both feet on the spiritual path.

As we know, it is a long and narrow path to get to heaven, or to have and keep both feet on the spiritual path, but it is certainly not impossible. Many people have done it, and many people are still doing it. It is only as difficult as we make it, or as easy as we make it, but it doesn't have to be as difficult as some people think it is.

Once someone has managed to get a foot on the spiritual path, and then he or she has reached the place of happiness, prosperity, and love. Once you get a taste of it, you will not want to turn back. Who would want to?

You are on your way to glory, so you just keep on striving to get deeper into it. As you see the light at the other end of the tunnel, as it keeps getting bigger and brighter, you want to reach it so much, because you feel happy and you feel so glorified, you don't want to look back, and you shouldn't.

But you have to be careful, be on your guard at all times, because it is easy to fall prey to temptation. Unfortunately, some people make the mistake of looking back and falling for temptation. These people are usually called *backsliders*. How we would love to bring them back on the right path again.

It is up to each individual to make his or her own decision. Whether we like it or not, we can't decide for anyone. But, fortunately, some do get back on the right path, because they want that freedom and that glorified feeling again. They want it so much that they can't live without it. That is when we should reach out and help them get back on the right path, the path to prosperity and happiness.

Someone once said that it is harder to get on the right path the second time than it was the first time. Well, whether it is the case or not, why take the chance? There is no point in it; it is a dangerous chance to take. So I say, once you get your feet on the spiritual path, don't look back, just keep on striving for more truth about the reality of life, and you will reach your goal.

You may think sometimes that I am persistent on certain subjects, but I have reasons for being so; it is far too important, and I can't help but be persistent. I believe that persistence pays off in many cases, if it is expressed properly, and at the proper time, especially when helping others.

We can only achieve happiness and glory if we are persistent in reaching our goal. We know that so many people lack enough dedication and persistence; therefore, they can never reach their destination or the goal that they have set to reach in their life.

Most of the time, it could be so easy and just right at their fingertips. They don't even know it, but with some dedication and persistence, success would open up right in front of them.

The sad part of it is that they will never know how close they were to starting to benefit from it all and how close they were to starting to feel happy because of their success.

Parents are persistent with their children for a good cause: parents want their children to have a successful future after they become adults. But after children become adults, it is up to them to be persistent, to become successful in their lives.

When children become adults, then they in turn also are

persistent with their children for the same reasons. It goes on and on, parents after parents, generation after generation, and the more a person persists in reaching his or her goals, the greater that person's chance of becoming successful in life.

A person who becomes successful in his or her life is a person who uses the tools (mentioned in Chapter 1) that are much needed to become successful. Those tools are used with proper persistence, at the proper time, with themselves and with others. These are all very good quality tools that are for everyone to use persistently.

Using tools involves intelligence, and develops more intelligence in a person's mind.

Some of us believe that some people are more lucky then others, but the truth is that an intelligent person has better chances to succeed in life because of the decisions that person makes.

An intelligent person will guide his or her life in a different way than a person who is not so intelligent; therefore, the one who is more intelligent is more likely to make a better decision, at the proper time, and for a good reason.

Intelligence gives a person a sense of making the right decision at the right time and at the right place; therefore, an intelligent person is more likely to get more or better chances in life than others are. They seem to be luckier than others are, but that is not necessarily the case. Even though it may seem that way to others, it is not always by luck, because most of the time, it is dedication, effort, and willingness that brings success to people.

Someone once told me that I was very lucky, because I had a beautiful family, I own my own house, and everything was well with my family and me, and so on. But my reply was that it wasn't because of luck, it was just because I had made a plan and made it my goal to reach. I was persistent and never quit. I became successful in reaching my goal; therefore, now I have what I've been working toward achieving. So that wasn't luck, I just got off my butt, went to work, and stayed persistent about it because I knew that it was an intelligent thing to do to reach my goal in my life, and I did.

Intelligence will bring a person to success and prosperity, both physically and on the spiritual path.

We should remember that people who have lots of money are not necessarily intelligent. We can easily see the difference between someone who is intelligent and has lots of money, and someone who has lots of money just by chance or by luck as we say. But some people can become successful and have lots of money, because they are intelligent enough, but they are not intelligent enough to know how to manage their success. Many times, these people will end up flat broke and at the bottom of the barrel, as we say. It is just because they were not intelligent enough to be able to control it properly, and they end up losing it all in the end.

Remember that money isn't everything, but it surely helps with our physical survival. It is surely needed to survive in this world, but intelligent people will not let money control their life, even though they may have lots of money or lots of belongings and properties.

We often see rich people who possess lots of money and live a long and very happy life. On the other hand, we also see people who possess lots of money and are not happy. Sometimes, some of those people even die young, sometimes by sickness or disease, and sometimes even by suicide. It is a very sad thing to see happen to anyone.

I hope you see the picture: the one who is rich with lots of money, and lives a long and happy life is a person who uses intelligence the right way in life. But the one who has lots of money, but is not happy, and dies young suffers from not being smart or intelligent enough to cope with life the proper way; they let money control their lives. A person could live a short and miserable live, while others could live a long and happy life. Having lots of money or being rich isn't always success for everyone. A person who fails to use intelligence properly in his or her life could live a short and miserable life if money or riches control their lives. We have to be careful about it, because we all know that we need money in our lives; but intelligence and happiness should come first. If there is no happiness in life, then money doesn't mean anything. In fact, sometimes money destroys happiness; it may even destroy lives.

Therefore, everything we do should be done with the power of love for ourselves and for everyone else also, because it is a universal law. It is the will of God that we do so, and doing the will of God is the most intelligent thing anyone can do.

Remember that when we do the will of God, we are rewarded openly. Jeremiah 31:16. These are the words of God and they can't be changed.

Universal law, or God's law, cannot be changed by anyone. God Himself won't even go back on His word, so how could we?

Jesus said to love everyone as you love yourself. Even though it may seem difficult at times, one has to realize and accept God's law, and make an effort to act according to the will of God, and he or she will be rewarded openly. I say it is a very profitable effort. Wouldn't you agree?

Anyone who can do that is a very intelligent person who uses his or her intelligence the right way, and for the right purpose. Therefore, a great reward is awaiting anyone who can live this kind of life, and this reward is overflowing with joy and happiness. This is real success.

We very well know that our brother, Jesus, was a very intelligent man. He has proven it in many different ways. We also know that without intelligence, He wouldn't have been able to do all the marvelous things that He did. We know that intelligence was one of His strongest tools, if not the strongest.

Jesus, just like us, had all the tools that He needed, to use for Himself and for everyone else also. But the only difference is that He used those tools that were given to Him by His Father. He was intelligent enough to understand them, knew what they were for, and how to use them properly, for the right purpose, and at the proper time. But, most importantly, He was willing to use all of these tools (as I call them) not just for Himself, but also for everyone else, because of the great love that He had for all of us. We know that His Father had sent Him to teach us, but we also should realize that He also could have refused to carry out the duty given to Him by His Father. But, because of the tremendous love that He had for all of us, He would never have refused the task.

Jesus had enough intelligence to know that it was best for everyone to carry out His Father's will, even though He knew the cost, the pain and the agony, and all the suffering that was on the road ahead for Him. His intelligence helped Him accept, or guided Him to accept, the tremendous task, and gave Him the will and strength to carry on without ever looking back.

With no regrets, Jesus accepted the task and made it His goal to reach. He wasn't about to even think of turning back, because His focus was on carrying on no matter what the cost to reach His goal. He did, all because of the love that He had for His heavenly Father, as well as for us. He wouldn't ever refuse to do His Father's will, because He knew very well that it was the right thing to do, and He understood that it was to benefit us all.

Therefore, we understand how important it is to be an intelligent person, because we know how powerful intelligence really is.

This teaching can be found in the first four books of the New Testament. There is much to learn in these four books, which are, Matthew, Mark, Luke, and John. Consulting these books is a very wise thing to do, because we all need learning. These texts are some of the best things we could ever learn. Also, the New Testament teaches a great deal about the reality of life, and we desperately need to understand it.

Now I would like you to stop reading for a while, and concentrate and study what you've read until now. Make certain that you properly understand what you've read before reading any further into the next chapter. I would like you to go back as far as you think you should go, maybe right from the very beginning, and read it all again, if you feel that you need to do so. Please be honest about it; take your time going through it to make sure that you don't leave anything behind or miss anything. I promise that you will be happy that you did.

Please stop now.

Review: Chapter 3, Intelligence

Intelligence was the topic of this chapter, and a very important topic it is.

We all know that intelligence is one of the biggest pieces of the puzzle in our life. We also know that, because of all the works that Jesus did using all the intelligence that He possessed, including all that's captured in His teachings, we have no choice but to learn from His great teaching. There are absolutely no excuses.

We know that some people develop intelligence earlier in their lives than others, but it isn't because one person is smarter then the next one. Some of us develop intelligence in a different time in life, and some at a different pace, but that certainly doesn't mean that one person is smarter than the other is.

I have to say that, in some cases, some people do get very intelligent, and for the right reason or for a very good reason, while others still get very intelligent, but unfortunately, not for such good reasons after all. Even though they truly believe that they are really very intelligent for the right reasons, in my view, it is only because of what they were taught in universities, to become whatever they wanted to become, in whatever field that they wanted to work in their future. Therefore, they learned what they were taught, they graduated, and they received the intelligence that they needed to work, in whatever field of work they were learning for. They succeeded in reaching their goal for their future. However, we have to admit that some of these intelligent people are in a position that they don't understand any other way but their own way, and no one else's way at all. In so many cases, it is very sad to see, and even to experience, because we very well know that many thousands of innocent people are getting killed all over the world, and because of some very intelligent people that govern the world. It is so sad that it makes me sick just to think of how many people that we try so hard to help to keep alive every day, while others are getting people killed just for the sake of selfishness.

These people are intelligent enough to become leaders of a country, making all kinds of promises, but they are not intelligent enough to keep their own people safe and alive, especially with all the technology that we have today.

But, fortunately, there are many people that do get educated and really use their intelligence for different reasons. For example, doctors, scientists that do research seeking a cure for cancer, theologians, and so on, people who are trying so desperately to find ways to make this world a better place to live. Well, these people I call my heroes, and I pray for them so that they can reach their goals. May God bless them with their research and other work so that they can succeed with their work and efforts.

Intelligent parents will usually encourage intelligence in their children also, and in the proper manner. When these young people become adults, then they too can teach their own children the same way so that they in turn can have a bright future ahead of them, and so on, generation after generation.

There are also some people who are born intelligent, and sometimes their intelligence guides them the wrong way in their lives. They can be very intelligent in whatever they do, but that doesn't mean that they are doing the right thing. It takes a very intelligent person to become the leader of a certain gang, but that doesn't mean that it is a good gang; it may be a gang of troublemakers, murderers, or B&Es, or anything that's no good. These so-called intelligent people are not so intelligent after all, because in the end, they will have nothing.

But there are intelligent people who are out to help people in any way they can, and these people will be rewarded and recognized forever, for the good that they have done for the whole society.

Chapter 4

Learning

Learning is one of the most important things in our lives, as we know, but what is in learning?

There are lots of things that we can learn in our lives, and fortunately, we learn lots of good things. But unfortunately, there are lots of things that people learn in their lives that are not so good. The outcome of this misdirected learning creates lots of problems for others, for themselves, and in fact, for the entire civilization.

We know that some people spend lots of their time studying and learning how to do things that are not beneficial for society, and in turn, not beneficial for themselves either. These people can become very intelligent but for the wrong purposes, while others are spending their time studying and learning good things for themselves, their family, and for the whole human race.

The ones who strive to learn for their own good and for the good of society are called value producers, and these value producers are successful in life.

Value producers start learning when they are very young children. They are integrated thinkers who start nursery school, and they go on to kindergarten, and they are very happy to move up to grade 1, then 2, and 3, and so on. These children are learning well, and they strive to reach grade 12 and graduate from high school and reach their goal.

These children have worked hard on learning for those years to get somewhere in their lives, and they are happy with their achievements. They have done something of which they can be proud.

These children have worked hard to reach their goal of graduating from high school. Once they reach that goal, then they have another goal in their mind that they want to reach, and it is to go to university and take on a certain trade, a trade that will bring them a good income in their future. Ultimately, they, like others, have and raise their own families the best way they can and find happiness in their future.

With a well-paid career, they can reach their goal in having a sufficient income for raising their children, and then putting them through the proper schooling. They help their children through university and help them reach their goal also, as they did themselves, so that one day, they can also be proud of their children's achievements.

When this happens, then they have reached success in their lives, and also in their children's lives. But, in the meantime, their children also have worked hard to reach their own goals. We know that it takes years of dedication and hard work for their children also, and they will reach their goals because they have received the proper guidance from their parents. They can be proud of their parents, and their parents can be proud of them. That brings happiness in their lives, because of their success and prosperity.

The same thing goes for spirituality. It is a process of learning, integrated thinking, and discipline, thought, and controls (D.T.C.).

This brings intelligence, knowledge, and wisdom. Only then

can a person walk on the spiritual path, and only then can a person know and experience spirituality.

Learning can be easy and lots of fun or it can be difficult. It is all up to each individual.

Let me give you an example. Sometimes, we can learn things without even trying, but it doesn't mean that it is a good or bad thing to learn. Sometimes, a person just wants to learn bad things, and they think that they are happy with their learning. But if it isn't for their own good and for the good of society, then they will not find happiness in it. They don't really know what real happiness is; therefore, they don't know what they are missing in their lives, and even though they believe that they have happiness in their lives, they really don't.

If a person is intelligent enough, and wants to learn new things or new ways in their lives, then they can find whatever is good or bad to learn, but it is up to them to make the proper decision. By making the proper decision, they find happiness, true happiness, in their lives.

As I mentioned in Chapter 1, if you are willing and determined to do good for society, as well as for yourself, you'll find happiness and prosperity in your life. It is because you are on the right side of society. If so, society is also on your side, too, and if society is on your side, you can't help but succeed and prosper with joy and happiness in your life.

Sometimes, people may think that they aren't very smart, or even think that they are not smart enough to do certain things. Sometimes, they give up on things, because they don't think that they can do anything worth doing or they think they could never do as well as the next person.

In reality, all that these people have to do is to be willing to learn and believe in themselves. Most of us can learn as well as anyone else, but some people just don't believe that they could do as well as anyone else. As I mentioned in the first chapter, it is lack of faith in oneself, but sometimes it is just because a person is puzzled by seeing the success, prosperity, and happiness that appears to be in someone else's life. These people don't believe in themselves enough to even think that they also could do just as well.

All that these successful people did was believe in themselves remain determined to learn, and become more intelligent.

I believe that most everyone has intelligence, but lots of people don't think that they are intelligent at all. It doesn't take very much intelligence to just know that people must make an effort and use discipline to reach their goal in life. I have to say that if someone knows this fact and still doesn't want to do anything about it, well, then I believe that it is because of laziness. There aren't any rewards in being lazy. Earlier, in the first chapter, I spoke about the ugly disease of laziness and what to do about overcoming it. But if you don't remember enough about it, then I strongly suggest that you go back and read from the first chapter again. Study it properly so that you can understand it and, very importantly, do whatever you can to remember what you've read. Perhaps you've read the text but have not really studied it. If you want this book to help you with your development, whether it is mentally, physically, or spiritually, you must make an effort in studying properly or the reading of this book will not have as much effect on you. Please take your time and do it properly. Learning about spirituality is far too important in everyone's life.

It isn't very difficult to read a book, but it is very different to really *study* a book. I know that many people think that they are able to understand everything that they've read, even if they've only read it once. However, if they were to read it the second time, they would realize that they had missed lots of very important points throughout the book, and they would be very happy that they have read it again.

As I've said, reading a book isn't very difficult to do, but to really study what you read takes mental work. A person must really understand what is read and store it in the mind so that it remains there forever. Information that was received from the study is still there and helpful to use whenever it is needed at any time, whether it may be to help you or to help someone else. It is developing intelligence, and it is very rewarding for anyone.

I have known some people who thought of themselves as being too smart or too intelligent to bother with almost any book, except for reading the Bible. Because they have read the Bible once or twice, and they don't really believe that any other book would help them, they don't really believe in reading any other books. They believe that they already know too much to read those books and that reading would be a waste of time. However, I can tell you that the truth is that they are missing the whole point altogether, and unfortunately, they are not as intelligent as they believe they are. It is really a sad thing to do.

It doesn't matter how we look at it; we all need intelligence to get anywhere worthwhile in life. But the best part of it is that it doesn't cost anything; it only takes the will to listen, learn, and obey, and it gradually grows in you. After a short time, you realize that you are getting more intelligent, because things seem to be easier to figure out than they used to be, and everything seems to go much smoother than before. It keeps getting better and better all the time.

You start seeing and understanding the truth about the reality of life, and you seem to see all kinds of things more clearly than you ever did before. That is all because of your learning. You are developing intelligence; therefore, you are getting rewarded for your efforts. Feeling happy because of the way you feel about yourself is just the beginning of your rewards.

We know that there are lots of very good and important books available to read and study. These books can help anyone in developing mentally, physically, and spiritually. However, I truly believe that it is much more profitable for anyone to read and study the Bible first, because it makes it so much easier to grasp the proper understanding about the reality of life and the real spiritual life, as it should be understood.

It is so very sad to see so many people all over the world who doesn't understand, who just can't put together the meaning of it all. They don't grasp the truth about what is real and what is not real in their lives, and they just can't see life as it is. Therefore, these people are living in spiritual darkness and just can't see the truth or the reality of it all. These people are oblivious to God's laws, including universal laws, and their purpose for everyone's benefit.

Anyone who is willing and determined to learn properly the things that are important to learn is bound to become successful. You can't help but to gain in intelligence, which means that you can't help but to become successful in your life.

As we should know, before making any effort in learning anything, we should be honest and positive about what we are about to learn, or about what we want to learn, to make absolutely certain that it would be something good to learn.

Learning something has to be for a future improvement or it is simply not worth learning. It would simply be a waste of time. Therefore, before learning anything, we should certainly be intelligent enough to know if it is worth learning or not.

Some people might say that we never know enough or too much, or the more we learn, the smarter we get. Well, I say that if we spend time learning things that are not necessary for us to know, then it would be much more intelligent to spend more time learning things that are of great value to us, wouldn't it?

Instead of wasting our time learning things that are really not of any value to us, especially if it is something that isn't going to help us in our future or to help someone else, then it is not worth learning. It's very simple.

Let us talk about something that can be valuable for us in our future, something that is worth all the efforts to learn, something that will bring us success, prosperity, and happiness. That is really something that is worth talking about.

We have talked about parents teaching their children, and children learning from parents, and learning from school, going up in grades and graduating from grade 12, going to university, and striving to become successful in their future.

Here we are talking about physical success, but in the truth about the reality of life, well, we all know that physical success is so very important in our lives, but it does make me feel good to say that spiritual success is by far more important. Whether some of us do believe this fact or not, it doesn't change the fact that it is the truth. Spiritual success is the best there is in everyone's life. Whether we understand this statement or not, it is the absolute truth. It is the reality of life, real life. It is God's universal law, and it cannot be changed or broken by anyone at any time.

Now let's go back to studying and learning. It is very wonderful to know that children can learn and grow up to become intelligent and successful adults, physically. But we have to realize that the real truth is that the same studies and practices go for learning about spirituality, too.

When children are very young, they usually go to church with their parents, often on Sunday. The parents get their children ready for church; they make sure that the children are well dressed and presentable to the public. That is also for a showing of respect to society, and at the same time, the parents know that it is also a great teaching of respect and dignity to and from their children. They know that their children will always remember these kinds of teachings and that they will grow up to be respectable people after they're on their own. They will also teach their children the same, and so the parents will be proud of their grandchildren as well as of their children. The children and grandchildren will know and remember the great teaching from their parents.

That's the way it should be for generation after generation, and it certainly should carry on in everyone's life forever.

While this is all happening, we have to realize that, usually, the parents know a lot more than we realize, because they do know and understand to a certain degree about spirituality. They understand enough about it to know that it is for the best for their children, so they get their children on the right track, as we say, and they try to teach them about spirituality as much as they can. Then they send them to catechism so that they can learn more about God, Jesus, all the saints, and about spirituality. They very well know that it will be very profitable to their children in their future, and they want their children to grow up intelligently so that they can become successful and live an honest and happy life. Then, they will be equipped to carry on the process into the next generation, and the next and the next.

We have to realize that it doesn't just stop there for these children. For these children, it is just the beginning. Their parents get them on the right track, but after they are old enough to be on their own, they have to take over on their own accord and continue this learning process on spirituality for themselves. They can't always depend on their parents to guide them by the hand. They have to go on their own and learn more, and as they do get older and smarter, it is much easier for them to understand. Therefore, it is also much easier for them to learn more about the reality of life and the true meaning of it all.

Learning about spirituality is not any more difficult than learning about anything else. It is like up grading yourself at school; you start at the bottom, and you work your way up. The more you learn at school, the more you go up in grades, until you reach your goal.

The same process applies to grading yourself with spirituality, and like schooling, you keep getting smarter and smarter, and it is surely lots of fun.

Therefore, your parents get you on the right track or on your feet spiritually as well as physically. After that, it is all up to you. You study your own Bible, you go to seminars, which are really lots of fun, you go to different denominations and meet very nice and pleasant people, and you make lots of new friends, and so on. But this is all because you really want to learn more about spirituality, because you find happiness in it. You get to understand it, and you also get to find the truth about the reality of life, as you should understand it. Because with all these people that you meet, you always study the word of God with them. You learn more than you could ever dream that you could, and the ones who know more than the others do teach the others and they are very happy to do so. But everyone learns from each other, and everyone is happy. It is just one big, happy family. These people are probably the best friends you could ever have, especially because of their honesty, and also because of the love that they want to share with you as well as with everyone else. You know that it is true love, and you want more of this joy and more of these great experiences. You don't want it to stop, ever, because it feels so good to love and to be loved by so many people.

In these kinds of places and with these kinds of people, you can't help but be happy. The more everyone learns about spirituality, then the happier everyone is, because spirituality is happiness, success, and prosperity.

Therefore, you are always anxious to meet your friends, and you also want to be able to give some help so that everyone can also learn from you. When you are alone, anytime during the week, during the day, whenever you have the chance, you can do your own learning. You can practice different things like talking with God, for example. Don't forget to listen to Him for His answers. You will be amazed at what you get in response if you really pay attention and listen carefully.

Remember that you can speak to God at anytime at all, when you're walking, working, eating, playing, whatever you're doing, use Him as your best friend and talk to Him every chance you get. You can even use Him as your helper if you want. Treat Him well, as if He was the best helper that you ever had, and the best friend you could ever have, and the experiences that you get you can share with your friends when you meet again. Can you just imagine if everyone would do that, how much everyone would learn in such a short time?

The best way to get on the spiritual path with God is to talk with Him, walk with Him, work with Him, and live with Him at all times. You will be rewarded openly, as He promised He would do for all His children, but we have to accept Him in our lives at all times. The question is why shouldn't we?

It is for our own benefit, after all. He is our Father, and He wants to live with us, do everything with us, and help us always.

There is no happiness greater than what you feel when you know that God is with you. He makes you feel the happiest that you could ever be, because He is happy to have you with Him. Just like a father with his loving child, there is no happier moment than a reunion with our heavenly Father.

We know that if God is happy with you, He will make you successful, prosperous, and keep you living in happiness for as long as you live with Him. He did just that with many other people, and still does the same today as He always did. He will also do it with you. It is also a promise that God made to His people, and we all know that He would never change His word, for His word lasts forever. Amen.

You learned from your parents and are now on your own. I believe that it is more fun studying about spirituality on your own free will and in your own way than it was when you were taught by your parents. It could be because you understand it better than before, and you have grown spiritually. Therefore, you enjoy it more and you also appreciate it much more than you ever did when you were younger.

You have found new, loving friends that you are very happy to be with, you know that your parents are happy with you because of the way you control your life, and now you should be able to share your experiences with your parents. They would also learn from you, some of the things that they probably wish they had known years ago, so that they could have thought you more than they did when you were young.

Now let's do a little exercise and see how you make out with it. Just close your eyes for a moment, and try to see in your mind yourself with your parents, brothers, and sisters. See how happy everyone is because of the happiness that they all received from understanding spirituality, and because they live with it every chance they get. See in your mind how the whole family is rejoicing together, and realize the wonderful role that spirituality plays in everyone's life. How beautiful it is, and what happiness it brings into the whole family and to your friends.

Now, if you are married and have children of your own, picture them with you among the rest of the family, and realize how much greater the joy and happiness is with everyone. Realize that with the help of your parents, you were able to bring this happiness to everyone in the whole family. This is because of your willingness to learn more about spirituality, by doing mental efforts, studies, and learning about spirituality after you were on your own. You can see that everyone is pleased with you, for your accomplishment. You have all the reasons to be happy with yourself, for your success in understanding the spiritual world, and the happiness there is in it. You also have received the great power of knowledge, while experiencing happiness with the whole family.

Hopefully, you were able to do this exercise and get the true feeling of spiritual happiness. You should also get some knowledge of it, but if for any reason you couldn't grasp that, then I ask you to practice it again until you get it right and you can do it properly. I certainly don't want you to miss this wonderful experience and the tremendous happy feeling that you would get from this exercise.

However, if you were able to do this exercise properly and had a taste of that great feeling, well, you should know that this is how it is for everyone who understands spirituality and lives according to God's will. As I've said before, you get all the success, happiness, and prosperity, and there is no mistaking it, because it is God's holy word.

Therefore, when someone is learning when they are young, and they keep on studying and growing spiritually after they become adults, and on their own, then there is no mistaking that this person does become intelligent and knowledgeable, and therefore, becomes successful in his or her life.

As we know by now, the answer to all of this is listen, learn, and obey.

Again, I would like you to stop reading and relax for a while. Concentrate on what you've read so that you can understand it better, before you go on reading into the next chapter.

Please stop now.

Review: Chapter 4, Learning

The word learning doesn't seem to mean much too some people, but it is only because they never really thought about what it really means. Perhaps they never considered the power that there is in learning.

Some people are really good learners, and some not so good, but that doesn't mean that a good learner will be better off than anyone else will. Sometimes a good and fast learner could become a leader of some bad club or a bad organization, and in a case as such, we could say that these people would be better off being very slow learners, and probably would be living a much better and happier life.

We all know that learning is a good thing, as long as it is learning something good for ourselves and also for the whole society so that we can all help each other in any way we can.

To be able to learn is really a great blessing. Therefore, we should use it for good purposes. It is the parents' duty to teach their children the proper things the proper way to get them prepared for their future, and so their children can teach their own children after that, and so on.

Children work very hard in learning to get to the next grade, graduate from grade 12, finish university, work hard in learning to get a good paying job, get married and have children, and with a good paying job to support their family, and they try everything they can to live a happy life with their family. Others like to spend most of their time learning something, anything negative, and because they really don't even know how great life could be if they were able or if they were given the chance to learn the proper things. Sometimes, it could be because that's what they want, but sometimes, it could also be because they never had the chance to know or understand any better; therefore, they don't always turn out on the right path.

Therefore, let me say this: whenever we see a child who seems to be a good thinker, or a child who seems to like to develop things, then we should certainly see that this child is helped with his mental development as much as possible, instead of just ignoring this child. This could be a very important breakthrough for this child, so he or she should be helped immediately.

I have also seen children who were very destructive, even at a very early age, and there were always so many problems with these children. That was probably because they didn't have the same ability to learn as others had.

Learning is very well needed if it is for the good for ourselves and also for the whole society.

Anyone that is willing and determined enough to learn properly, and for the good of everyone else and themselves is certain to become intelligent, and will certainly succeed and prosper in their lives.

Chapter 5

Knowledge

Knowledge is also a very important piece of the puzzle. There is a lot of power in knowledge; in fact, I believe that without knowledge, there wouldn't be very much, if any, good quality work done any time anywhere. We all know that with no quality in anything that we do, there wouldn't be very much anyone could hope for, humanly speaking, when it comes to success, prosperity, and happiness in anyone's physical or spiritual life.

Knowledge can be earned by working hard mentally and physically, practicing enough, studying and learning more about the truth of the reality of life and its purpose, and experiencing the goodness that abides in the true life itself. We certainly know that knowledge doesn't come without mental efforts and physical work.

Any job can only be properly accomplished, and properly completed, by someone who has the knowledge necessary to successfully get the job done in the proper manner and in the proper time span.

Knowledge comes from studying, learning, and practicing on any task taken. We shouldn't say that we could do a certain job properly, or as well as anyone else could, unless we have already done it. The more times we perform a task, the more knowledge we have on that certain task, and the more knowledge we have on that task, the better we can accomplish the task and complete it properly in the proper time span.

That knowledge is what makes a person a professional at what he or she does. A person who has the *profession* to do a certain job usually gets paid more than anyone else who simply performs the task, because he or she has the knowledge necessary to do the job properly, in the proper time, and for a proper cost for whomever the job is done.

These people deserve to get paid more than others get, because they have spent lots of time studying, learning, and practicing to gain the knowledge necessary to get to where they are with their profession. If they have done all this preparation in a positive way, and it is for the good of society as well as themselves, then it is a good and honest profession that is worth all the efforts to learn and afterward earn a good pay for doing it.

We also know that the more knowledge we get, the more intelligent we become. These powerful tools have been used by many people all over the world throughout the years, and by using these powerful tools, people can't help but have success and prosperity in their lives.

Right now, you might be asking yourself, what is he getting at, where is he going with this, or what does this have to do with spirituality? But, let me tell you, it has everything to do with spirituality, as you'll find out in the next chapters, from verbalization to examples, taught by the King of Kings, our brother and Lord Jesus Christ, the light of the world.

Someone can become very knowledgeable after spending lots of time studying, learning, and practicing different things in different ways.

Let us suppose that a man is interested in a specific job, and he feels that he would really like this job if he knew how to do it properly. So he goes on to study about it, learn it, and practice it. He is determined to succeed with his plan and won't quit or look back for anything. Ultimately, he succeeds with his plan, and he becomes devoted to the job that he enjoys doing. He gets so good at it that he becomes a real professional in his field, because he became very knowledgeable through all the studies, learning, and practice that he put into it. In the end, it pays off very well, because he could become an entrepreneur of a very successful business or simply enjoy his work.

We have to remember that if people really like the job they have and enjoy doing it well, then they can't help but become successful with it. But, remember that the most important part of work is if people find happiness in their job. If they are happy, they will be successful, because happiness is success.

Knowledge can be much more important in someone's life then we realize. Knowledge is not only good for operating a successful business or becoming a well-known celebrity, even though it is very important to have these kinds of things in our lives. But it is also very important for helping us reach a good understanding about spirituality and the truth about the reality of life. Whether we understand and realize this fact to be true doesn't change the fact that it is a very true statement. It cannot be changed by anyone. It is a reality in our lives, and it should be understood, accepted, and dealt with as is by everyone. There is no exception.

From studying the word of God from our Bible and other great books, we understand that, for some people at a certain time in their lives, it is important for them to fall into a lower stage, if I can put it this way, meaning that they get into problems, lots of problems sometimes. These people suffer to the point that they feel that there is no way out. They struggle and struggle, living in misery for some time, until after such long time living in this miserable life, and when there seems to be absolutely nothing left to do, then suddenly something wonderful happens. They start using their mind properly, start thinking properly, and do some hard, integrated thinking to find a way out of this hard time. They suddenly realize that the only thing left to do or to try is to turn to God and ask Him to help because there is absolutely nothing else left to try. To their surprise, He was always right there to help. They realize that God was always there, waiting for them to call on Him for help. But, sadly enough to say, once again, He was last when He should have been first. He would have helped anytime, especially before all of these problems and hard times started.

Many times, the only way people will acknowledge God, or try God for help, is when there is absolutely nothing else left to try. Many times, this is the only way that someone gets to know God and understand His purpose. But, even though they left Him behind for so long and completely ignored Him for so long, He never forgets anyone, is always ready and willing to forgive anyone at any time, and is always by our side, willing and ready to help.

From that time on, these people go on living a better and happier life, and they never forget what God has done for them. They go on living a more spiritual kind of life than ever before, because of what they have experienced in the past, with all the struggle they lived through and the knowledge they received from all the hard times, and because of the miracle of having their lives turned around, from poverty, struggle, and living in misery to happiness and success with the help of God. Their knowledge is anchored by the realization that there was a God they could turn to in times of need, a God who was there during all times.

With the knowledge that they now have, they will not likely fall into the same situation again. They are very thankful because they have experienced the beauty and the wonderful power that there is in God. For the rest of their lives, they praise God every chance they get because of the happiness that they have now. They are living in a totally different world, a happy world, a more promising way of living, the best of all worlds; they have found a world of spirituality where everything is possible for everyone at anytime.

Sometimes, it seems, people must acknowledge the living at the bottom of the barrel, as we say, before they can achieve success by getting to know God.

Therefore, knowledge is a very important and powerful tool, or gift and ability, that everyone desperately needs and should have.

Speaking for myself, I honestly can say that I have also received lots of very good experiences and knowledge for many years of my life, by sometimes living an upstream battle, and again, sometimes living a downstream success, in reaching whatever goal I set myself to reach.

Therefore, I did have some failures, but by the grace of God, I always managed to recover from those failures. Also by His grace, I've succeeded with plans I have made and goals I have set for myself to reach, and I very well know that without God's help, I wouldn't ever have reached any of my goals. I wouldn't ever have seen success in so many plans that I have made for myself to follow if I hadn't turned to God for help.

Many years ago, I realized and decided that I didn't have to be rich to be happy, even though I would have liked to have lots of money, as most people would like to have. But I understood that love and happiness had to be first, because with love and happiness, there is success. The truth is I just couldn't see how I could ever become rich, not by far anyway.

So I decided that if I never will be rich, with money that is, then I know that I can make myself happy by becoming successful in different things that I set myself to do. I envision a plan to make and made it my goal to reach, and did whatever was necessary to do to reach my goal, even though that was just something small sometimes. I knew that I would be happy because of my success, but as I've said before, I also had some failures.

Even though I had some failures, those experiences weren't entirely failures, because I have decided that if I fail on certain things, then I will just use that as an experience to help me succeed the next time I worked on reaching another goal. Surprisingly enough, I didn't get so angry, depressed, or hurt because of a little failure when one would happen. I realized that I was getting some very good learning experiences. I also realized that I was getting smarter, because after a while, I was taking on bigger tasks for my goals. I would succeed more often than before, but the best part was that I was happy, and that is all that I needed to keep going in life. As long as I was happy, everything else should go well for me. After so long now, I can say that things turned out right for me. The truth is that I was getting smarter, and I also was becoming more intelligent from all of this success and failure.

This is a true message, and I hope that it will help you with your study. This message was and still is a reality in my life. It has been very helpful to me, and I know that it can also be of great help to you also. Please pay close attention to what you're reading and concentrate on it carefully. It is so very important to you to realize and understand.

You see, I didn't just give up on things because of a little failure. No, instead, I used a failure as a good experience to upgrade myself, so that I could make things get better in my life. Things did get better, and they are still getting better. I feel good about myself, and I have the right to feel this way. It is one of my successes. I know that you can do the same and feel good about yourself, after each time you succeed—even if the success is in the guise of a failure carrying a life lesson.

We have to remember that it is this kind of feeling that brings people to have faith, in God as well as in them. This feeling brings people great success and happy living, being in harmony with yourself, with God, with your entire family, and with the whole society included. The power of love in action in your life; therefore, you just can't fail.

Remember D.T.C., as you studied in the second chapter. Work with it, practice it, and watch the great results happening in your life.

Now I would like you to stop reading for a while, relax for as long as you want, and when you feel that you are ready, and then I would like you to review this chapter very carefully. It is very important to read this chapter time and time again, to get the proper feeling about it and to make sure that you didn't leave anything behind. Make sure you understand the whole chapters properly before you go into the next chapter. This is important so that you can put this great piece of the puzzle in its proper place, to form the great picture that we will be able to see at the end of your studies.

Remember that you don't have to stop reading only when I ask you to stop. You can stop as often as you want. Stop any time that you feel that you should stop, for whatever the reason is, and continue whenever you feel that you are ready to continue studying.

You know better than I do how much you can take and when you are ready to continue.

Please stop now.

> Jesus said in the book of Mark, 3:35: whosoever shall do the will of God, the same is my brother, and my sister, and mother.

Review: Chapter 5, Knowledge

Knowledge, as we know, comes with hard work. We can only become knowledgeable with some things that we work with, and the more we work with them, the more knowledgeable we become. With enough knowledge, we get successful in what we do to make a living.

Sometimes, people will say that they know how to do certain job, but in reality, they really don't know unless they've already done it. In Chapter 4, we covered a great area on this subject, because of its importance.

Chapter 6

Power of Love

Our brother, Jesus Christ, is probably the best one that we can use for an example to describe love and its power. We all know that Jesus had all the love and intelligence that anyone could have, while He was here on Earth among us in His physical and visible form, teaching us the truth about life, physically and spiritually.

Jesus wasn't just a storyteller or someone who wanted to be a leader, making up stories so people would look up to Him and follow Him.

Jesus was a true king, a king of the most high, and He wouldn't settle for anything but the truth in everyone's life.

He experienced life and death here on Earth with compassion, faith, love, and strength. He understood what was going on with the leaders of the world, and with the rest of society, and He wanted to set things straight. He wanted to set the society free, free from the burden of lies in the world that were keeping society in darkness or blindness of the real truth.

Jesus had it all at the fullest: love, intelligence, passion, wisdom, strength, knowledge, faith, courage, success—you name it, He had it. He was perfect, as His Father wanted Him to be perfect, and it was all because of the love that was to be shared with everyone.

This love that Jesus had when He was here with us visibly and physically wasn't just any kind of love. It wasn't a love like when two people fall in love with each other, have sex, and afterward, have children. Of course, that kind of love is a very wonderful thing and a necessity in our lives.

The love that Jesus had, and still has and lives with, is much greater than that kind of human love. It is a pure love, an unbreakable, undeniable love, a love that means power, intelligence, loyalty, passion, obedience, strength, wisdom, knowledge, forgiveness, and so forth. This pure love is strong enough to understand the universal law and to obey it to the fullest without the smallest unwanted spot or blemish whatsoever. It is a love that means power or ability to exist or to make exist, an ability to create or to bring into existence, and then the ability to take care of it all afterward for our benefit.

This love is strong enough that Jesus could use it to let Himself suffer to death on the cross and then bring Himself back to life, physically on the third day after His crucifixion, and then ascend to heaven to sit on the everlasting throne. Jesus had it all, used it all, and did it all for all of us. He sacrificed because of the tremendous amount of love that He had for us all, and still has for us all, so that we can always turn to him in times of need. I think that after all that He did for us, we could and should love Him enough to, at the very least, spend a little time speaking to Him every day. Whenever we have a chance, we should show our respect and thank Him for what He has done for us and what He is still doing for us all.

All that Jesus asks of us is that we love Him, believe in Him, and trust in Him with all our heart, mind, and soul. I don't believe that it is asking too much. We owe Him that much. I know that if we have love for Him and understand what real love is all about, and use some of that love for Him, and then we are certainly on the right path, the road to glory. We would get there by the power of love and only by the power of love, because there is no other way, because love is life, and without love, there would be no existence. Therefore, we have to thank God for giving us the power of love and teaching us how it will work for us if we put it into practice in our lives. If we work with it the proper way, with harmony with all society, we know that it would benefit the whole human race. That is the only way to succeed and prosper in life.

Jesus said love each other as I loved you. John 15: 12. We know that if we all did just that, there wouldn't be any wars and hatred as we witness every day in this world where we live.

That takes more love power then we could even imagine or dream of to do what Jesus did for us.

There was never before or never since as much truth coming out of anyone as it did from our brother, Jesus. Because He loved us so much, He allowed himself to spend this time of His physical life among the society to teach us the truth about reality of life here on this planet Earth. He did whatever He could to teach us about the creator of all creations and to implant the great wisdom into our mind, so that we could understand the real purpose of all the great creations that were created for all of us to benefit from.

Jesus didn't have to do all that He did, but He wanted to, because His interest was to teach us in a way that we could see and understand the truth about the reality of life at it's fullest. He wanted us to live a happy and prosperous life while we are here on Earth.

He said, "I am the light of the world." John 8: 12. He was trying to get people to see the truth in life; in other words, He wanted us to see the light at the end of the tunnel. Jesus was the open door to the truth about the reality of life, and He wanted us to realize this fact. He said, "I am the light." He wanted us to see Him as the real truth of everything and learn from it.

Jesus meant, if you trust in me, listen, and learn from my teaching, then you will clearly see and understand the truth about the reality of life and its true purpose for everyone to live by and to benefit from. Let me repeat His message: listen, learn, and obey, and by doing just that, we will become smart, wise, and intelligent.

He did everything that He could to get us out of darkness or blindness, to the point of suffering to death on the cross. Yet still, in this day and age, most of us remain blind of the truth.

I don't believe that anyone could teach us more effectively than Jesus did. That leaves us with the fact that if we want to live a good, happy, and prosperous life, physically and spiritually, then we just have to make the right decision, study, and obey His teachings as it was meant to be. Only then will we be able to see the light at the end of the tunnel; only then will we get the proper understanding of what Jesus meant when He said, "I am the light." When we really understand what He meant when He said those words, then we also understand the power that was in that short sentence. Jesus was no fool. He was always speaking with authority and power, but He always had difficulties gaining the understanding of His people and getting them out of darkness or blindness of the real truth about the reality of life.

Because of the power of love, Jesus never gave up on us. He fought against the lies and false pretense of the leaders of society until His death so that we could understand and see the true light of His message.

If we would just dedicate some of our time to study His teaching and to understand the true message He gave us, then we could start seeing the light that Jesus was talking about. We could start thinking about putting our feet on the spiritual path. Once we get on the spiritual path, then we should have enough intelligence to keep on walking on the spiritual path. If we keep the power of love in our mind and understand what it really is, then we can't help but succeed, prosper, and live in harmony with all humanity and the universe that is all around us.

As I've said before, there is no power greater than the power of love, because without the power of love, nothing would have been created. Without the power of love, there would be no existence here on Earth. All is love and from love.

Love is life, and not only human life, but the life of all that exists here on Earth and in the universe.

We need to have the proper intelligence to understand the power of love and its purpose. When we get to understand what love really is and live according to the power of love, not only for ourselves but also for all humanity, then we are also living with the power of wisdom. Without wisdom, we wouldn't have the ability to understand and feel the power of love for what it really is.

Love is also the greatest thing to share with anyone, because sharing love with someone else is really sharing life with someone else. Sharing good information or sharing work, helping out anyone who is in need of a helping hand, is really sharing life with someone else, too. Remember that anyone who can live this kind of life with society is someone who just can't fail in his or her life. This person is living in harmony with society and can't help but succeed and prosper.

Therefore, before one knows what love really is and understands how to live by it, one must develop intelligence. With this puzzle piece put into practice, then we start receiving wisdom. Then comes the proper understanding of what the power of love really is. Only then can one see and recognize the true light at the other end of the tunnel.

Anyone has the same right and authority if we have the desire and the will to use this power. It is for our own glory, and it is also for the glory of our God, for glorifying our God is glorifying us also.

Jesus said in anything and everything that you do, do it in the glory of God, I Corinthians 10- 31, which is our Father in heaven, and our Father, which is in heaven, will reward you openly. Jesus knew what He was saying. He knew that if anything we do is done in the glory of our Father, which is in heaven, then all is done with the power of love and truth.

We cannot fail, because we are all children of God the Father. When we do anything to glorify our Father, then we already know that our Father will reward us openly, with exceeding rewards above and beyond our expectations. That puts us all in the same family, the family of love. Everyone in this family shares all powers and abilities.

We're all member of the family of the same God, sharing the same powers and abilities, if we only open our hearts to our Father and glorify Him that controls all of our needs. He is always willing and ready to pour out His glory upon us from His storehouse. All we need to do is ask and believe that we have already received, and give thanks, knowing that it is already ours. It is, but we have to believe with all our heart, mind, and soul, without a doubt, and we have received.

I know that it may be easier said than done, but if you meditate on it and practice, before you know it, you will start feeling that something good is happening inside of you, that something is changing and you start feeling happier. You start feeling the power of love working inside of you.

Keep practicing on your mental focus on good and love for all society, and keep pressing on. If something else comes into your mind at times, reject it, get it out of your mind, and start again. Practice more; as we say, practice makes perfect. The more you practice, the better it gets. Before you know it, you start getting into the stage of knowing, which is beyond believing.

When someone doesn't understand this reality, then one has to practice his or her belief and as I have already said. While you are practicing that you believe that you have already received and that you start feeling a happy change that is occurring inside of you, then you know that there is something real in it. You have received the proof that it is really true; therefore, you don't only believe, but you know because you have experienced the power of love in action.

If you have been reading without stopping for a while, I suggest that you stop reading a while and concentrate on what you have already read. Make sure that you understand the messages properly before you read any further. There is no point in reading any further if one doesn't have the proper understanding of it all. Make sure that you are able to put all the puzzle pieces together up until now, and without any mistakes, and be certain that you are able to do it properly before reading any further. Please be honest about it, because it is for your own benefit.

Please stop now.

> Love and be loved, and I say I love you even if you think you
> don't love me.

This is another big piece of the puzzle, and as we keep on putting more pieces together, you will begin to see the whole picture. You will find the answers to your questions by the time that you finish reading and studying this book. You will understand what the truth about the reality of life really is, and then you will feel the power of wisdom building up inside of you. You will walk on the spiritual path, with peace of mind, and with your heart full of joy and happiness. You will not only believe, but you will also *know* that you are going the proper way in your life, the way to glory. There will be no stopping you because you will be living your life in joy, love, success, prosperity, happiness, and glory. You will be living in harmony with the rest of society as you never had done or seen done before in your entire life. There will be no turning back for you, no looking back for anything else. You will have your feet on the spiritual path, and you'll be walking straight forward.

But before we get to that point in our life, we have to use and practice the tools I have described in the previous chapters. There is no other way to reach that point, but it really pays off. Remember that practice brings success; practice makes perfect.

Dedicate yourself to honest study, learning, and practice, and don't give up, because that isn't something that anyone should quit. Be wise. Use the great power of wisdom; it is far too important, and anyone that would give up on this is someone who would give up on the reality of life. This person would remain in darkness or blindness of the truth about the real life. It would be sad to see anyone give up on such an important factor in life.

Practice with all your heart, mind, and soul, with love in your heart for all the world and the world will know. As I have mentioned before, everyone will know because they will feel the power of love and happiness flowing from you, and they will love you in return. We can't help but prosper and succeed in our life, because no one can fail with the power of love.

The real truth is "love never fails." God is love and God never fails. 1 John 4: 8.

Amen.

Review: Chapter 6, Power of Love

In this chapter, we've talked about some very important issues concerning the power of love.

We all already know that there isn't any power stronger then the power of love. Therefore, it is to be taken and handled in a very special way, because without love, there wouldn't even be any existence to begin with.

With and from the power of love, Jesus did everything that He did for us. He suffered to death just because of the love that He had for all of us.

Love is everything, love is life itself, and love is for everyone to live with and to live by. Share the power of love with anyone else, and anyone else will share the power of love with you, too. As we've talked about in previous chapters, love is free, and it is to be shared with others freely.

Chapter 7

Wisdom

Let's just say, lovely. Here we have just found another great piece of the puzzle: wisdom.

Now let's just sincerely think for a moment. A wise person is a person who can become rich, successful, prosperous, happy, intelligent, and so on. Just thinking about it feels wonderful, doesn't it?

Thinking about wisdom inspires us to become wiser, so that we too can become all those things. We wish to live a happy life like anyone else that we see sometimes, very happy and successful people who seem to have real peace of mind. It seems as if nothing or nobody bothers them, no matter what anyone says to them or about them. It is just because they are wise enough to not let anything or anyone gets the best of them, as we say, mentally, physically, emotionally, or spiritually. We know that anyone that does practice that kind of self-control is already a wise person. We also know that this person will eventually be like the others we just talked about, those who are happy and successful and have no worries in life.

Wisdom is a very high degree of power that brings knowledge. Therefore, wisdom is another great piece of the puzzle that needs to be seen, understood, and put into its proper place before one can start to see the whole picture. When we become wise people, we can't fail; we can only succeed in life.

Therefore, wisdom is something anyone can work on developing. It is not only for certain people; it is for anyone who is ready and willing to take action. It takes a certain amount of concentration, dedication, practice, and D.T.C., and in a little while, you start feeling that something good is happening inside of you. You start feeling good about it, and then you start understanding all about the great reward that is coming to you for your work and efforts. Let me tell you that it is a reward that is well deserved by anyone who is willing to make some sacrifices to reach their goal in life.

We know that when our brother, Jesus, was among us here on Earth in His physical body, He did all His work and all with perfection because of His wisdom, and with the wisdom that He had, there was nothing that was impossible to Him.

Jesus was constantly willing to perform all kinds of wonders and miracles for the entire world to see, so that we could learn from His teaching. We know that there was no mistaking in His teaching.

He was perfect and made no mistake. He knew what He was talking about, and He also very well knew what He was here to do. He was also aware of the rough journey that was ahead of Him, but still, He never backed out from anything. He faced everything with the great power of wisdom; this power gave Him the strength that He needed to perform His tasks, because with the power of wisdom, He was able to visualize and understand the rough journey that was ahead of Him. He was also able to see right through the real purpose of this journey, and because of all the great qualities, abilities, and powers, along with His will to obey His heavenly Father, He was able to accept and carry on that tremendous task that no one else would want to face. But our brother, Jesus, accepted it with no fear, no doubt, no regrets, and most of all, no plan in changing His mind for any reason whatsoever. Jesus had enough wisdom to really see and understand what was in the real power of love for the entire world. He wasn't about to ever turn back for anything, and He wasn't about to settle for anything less than the truth for all humanity.

Jesus came to speak the truth and spread the good news to the entire world. His wisdom enabled Him to do all that He did with perfection.

He had intelligence, love, wisdom, and strength, and by the will of our Father in heaven, He did perform all His duties as they were meant for Him to perform. He did it all with love, strength, wisdom, intelligence, and never with any intentions of looking back for any reason.

Jesus had a truthful heart, mind, and soul, and with the power of love that He possessed and all the wisdom that anyone could possibly wish to possess, He was able to teach us the truth about the reality of life. No matter what would happen to Him, He was willing to go through what He went through because He loved us with all His heart. Nothing was going to stop Him, and because of the wisdom that Jesus had, He knew beforehand what He was going to go through. Still, He never backed down from anything or anyone, because He had a duty to perform and that was our Father's will for Him to do so. We know very well that Jesus would never say no to our Father, because of the loyalty that He had for our heavenly Father and the love that He had for all of us, His brothers and sisters.

Jesus knew very well that the people were kept in blindness or darkness of the truth by higher earthly authorities with their lies, just because they wanted to keep control over humanity. I believe that our Father, which is in heaven, didn't like what was happening here on Earth, with the people that Himself had created, and that He was going to do something about it. Therefore, He sent His son, Jesus, to our rescue.

Our Father in heaven gave Jesus all that He needed to perform the task and sent Him here among us with all His wisdom to save us, to bring us out of blindness. Because He loved us that much, He gave His only begotten son to save us from the faults that humanity was living in and to free us from the grip of the higher earthly authorities. He freed us to see and experience the beauty of life, as it is meant to be experienced, by understanding the truth about the reality of life, as it was meant to be understood and lived, according to God's plan for all His children.

Jesus never backed down and never said no to any of His Father's requests, even though He knew what He was going to experience and that He was going to be crucified and suffer to death on the cross. He accepted the responsibility for the task, just because of the tremendous amount of love that He had for us.

If it wasn't for Jesus and all His intelligence, wisdom, and His will to do the will of His Father, we would be still living in a dark world with no hope to see the light and understand the reality of life as it was meant to be for us.

God created everything that He created for our purpose in our lives. We can't forget that He gave us the authority to command and use all of what He has created with no limitation. But, because we are still keeping ourselves so far in darkness, we still can't see or recognize these great abilities and authorities that we really have. I believe that our biggest problem is our lack of faith, faith in God our heavenly Father and faith in ourselves, as

Jesus spoke off so many times. It is because of lack of intelligence and wisdom that we remain blind in darkness of the real truth.

Lack of intelligence and wisdom is caused by the refusal to listen, learn, and obey. Study the word of God, and obey the word as it was meant to be learned and obeyed according to God's will.

God has made all the great gifts, powers, and abilities and has given them to all of us to use as He wants us to use them. But we are still to learn how to use all these abilities because we are still living in blindness. In other words, we are still spiritually blind, and it is not God's fault if we are unable to get out of this darkness and see the beauty of life. But for our lack of wisdom and faith, we would get to understand the reality of life.

If we just stop for a moment, take a good look at ourselves, and concentrate on what we've just discussed, then we could soon see that we are a weak nation. We also must admit that we are somewhat mentally lazy, even though it is sometimes very difficult to do. But, we should at least admit it to ourselves, because as long as we refuse to make a mental effort to do something about it and correct this situation, we can and will remain in this dark life. We will remain in the dark for as long as we want, all the while knowing we also could get out of it any time we wanted if we only have the will to do so.

Now I would like you to stop reading for a moment and concentrate on what you have already read. Make sure that you have the proper understanding and that you are able to start putting these puzzle pieces at their proper places before you read any further. It is better if it is done this way.

It is up to each individual how they read and study a book of such importance as this one, but I would say that if you feel satisfied with reading and studying two or three pages each day, or every second day, whatever you feel is better for you, by all means, it is OK by me. I know that it is much better to take more time to study something and do it properly, than to just go through it quickly and not get the proper understanding of it all. Therefore, please take your time and do it properly. I know that it will help you a great deal more this way, especially if you are working with honesty.

Please stop now.

We should understand enough now to know that with the proper wisdom and intelligence, nothing is impossible to us. With the proper wisdom and intelligence, we have the proper faith. But without faith, we can't do anything of high value, for ourselves or for anyone else in our lives.

Therefore, we have to realize that we must make some kind of mental effort. This effort is taking time to study the word of God carefully and making sure that we understand the true meaning of it. Once we grasp the proper meaning of it and we know that we understand it properly, then we have to obey it and put it into practice every chance we get. That way, we can get to experience the goodness of it all, and get to know how appreciative it is. It is the only way.

Now, putting the word of God into practice is done not only through speaking words, but also by living according to the word of God. It is His will that we do so. To do the will of God is to listen and obey, study the word of God, accept it, and practice it until you can live according to His will with joy and happiness to do so in your heart, mind, and soul.

While you are studying, learning, and practicing to live according to the will of God, you are gaining the proper strength, wisdom, and intelligence. It is very intelligent to study and practice, because that's when we receive the proper wisdom that we all need so very much. As I've said before, with wisdom, you receive faith, and with the proper faith, nothing is impossible to you. Our brother, Jesus, told us this truth so many times and in so many ways, while teaching us the truth about ourselves and the reality of life.

Therefore, as I see it, the key puzzle pieces, which I also like to call tools, to physical and spiritual development, prosperity, and success are love, intelligence, wisdom, and faith, just to name a few. Those are very powerful tools, and by using those tools, one cannot fail. If we use these tools properly, nothing is impossible to us.

It is a promise from God that so many of us seem to have so much difficulty understanding, but we have to remember that Jesus was very persistent on things that are very important for us to know and understand. In my view, there is no mistaking His teaching. Therefore, I have to say, Jesus said it, and that's good enough for me. In other words, He said it, and that settles it.

Remember that a wise person is a person who listens, learns, and obeys. Sometimes, a person need to discipline oneself and practice to stay quiet, listen, obey, and learn to become wise.

We know that wisdom is a word that carries a tremendous amount of power. It is wonderful to be able to understand what wisdom really means, and how wonderful it is to be able to live with this power. Lots of people would love to be wiser, or to be able to use the power that there is in wisdom, but unfortunately, not so many of us are willing enough to make the efforts and sacrifices needed to reach the mental ability to recognize and use this power. It is really sad, because it is worth all the effort and practice that a person can put into it. As I mentioned in Chapter 1, the reward is so great that if only we could visualize how tremendously rewarding it is, then maybe more people would be willing to use more of their time in studying and practicing on this subject. Then they, too, could reach this power and ability and live in harmony with it, as well as with the other great powers and abilities that we call tools, and live according to the will of God our Father for His glory and for ours also.

Now I would like you to stop reading and concentrate on what you've read until now.

See if you can properly place this puzzle piece at its proper place among the others, and if it seems too difficult to do, then I strongly suggest that you go back and read from Chapter 1 again. After you do that, you will be able to place it at its proper place with not so much difficulty. It is for your own benefit, and it is far too important to just take a chance and go on reading. You might miss the most important part of it all. Please take all the time that you need, and make sure to do it properly.

Remember that when it comes to the truth about the reality of life, I don't believe that anything is much more important than to really understand it all the way that it should be understood. Therefore, if you properly read and study something as important as the truth about the reality of life, with honesty and with an open heart and mind, then you can't fail. We know that it takes a wise person to do this properly. By being honest about it and doing it properly, then you will develop more wisdom. We never have too much wisdom, nor are we ever too wise.

The more we develop wisdom, the more we become intelligent. We also develop faith, and we become more successful in our lives with anything we do.

Therefore, please take as much time as you need and do it properly. It is for your own benefit.

Please stop now.

With faith and wisdom, nothing is impossible to us, and we know this because Jesus said so.

Review: Chapter 7, Wisdom

A very powerful word that is very well needed in everyone's life, in this chapter we talked about what it takes to become wise and what wisdom will do for us if we want it and understand it.

Wisdom is a tool that holds a very great amount of help to get us to the gates of heaven. Therefore, it isn't to be ignored at any time because it is far too important for everyone. Whether we do realize this fact to be true or not, it doesn't change anything, because it still and always will hold the same importance in everyone's life.

We also described a wise man, that is, a man who would keep his mouth shut, listen, and learn, while others are busy doing all the talking, even if sometimes whatever they say doesn't really mean much of anything. Therefore, a wise man is a man who can tame his tongue and spend more time thinking good and proper thoughts about everyone and everything. As we spoke of before, a wise man will use his mind only for good integrated thinking, and, therefore, good results will be produced from this good thinking. A wise man will not waste good thinking time on foolishness; wisdom is far too important to waste it on things of no importance.

Chapter 8

Faith

Faith—what a wonderful and powerful word! Second only to the power of love, I believe that faith is the most powerful tool and ability available for us to use. How I love and believe in this word. There is such a tremendous amount of power in faith. The amazing wonders never cease to grow among the believers of the gospel and its powers. Faith is a very true reality in life.

It is unfortunate that there are so many people in this world who still don't really understand the meaning of such a powerful word. How important it is for us to realize and recognize what the word faith really means for everyone. How important it is to appreciate the power it carries. Most important is our ability to use this power, for our own benefit and the benefit of all humanity.

True faith has brought very powerful physical and spiritual success to many people all over the world for many thousands of years. In fact, it has been a spiritual force since the beginning of time really, because people had, and lots of people still do have, the proper understanding of what true faith really is. They are willing to put it into practice, or work with it, if you will, because they very well know that by using this great power and living in harmony with it, they will have all that they need to succeed and prosper in their lives. They know that with true faith, they can have it all, and nothing can stop them from getting it all.

We all know that having enough faith to believe is something great, but having enough faith to have reached the stage of *knowing* is certainly something much greater. When you are in the stage of knowing, then nothing is impossible to you. As Jesus said in His teaching: in Matthew 17: 20. If you have faith even as small as the size of a mustard seed, then you can do anything you want and nothing is impossible to you; you can move mountains; you can stop the water flow or make it flow, as you will to do; you can bring prosperity and success into your life; and you can bring happiness in anyone's life, with the proper faith, nothing is impossible to you.

By believing His words, working on this message, and practicing it, that's when you start developing true faith. With true faith, one can do anything. Nothing is impossible to a person who believes enough to have the proper faith, and have enough faith to know.

This is a promise, and we have to believe that this promise will remain forever because it is directly from God himself. There is no mistaking it, for there is no mistaking that God's words contain everlasting love and truth.

Now, I would like you to pay very close attention to what you are about to read in the next few pages. It will help you understand what true faith really is and what it can do for you, from physical to spiritual walk in your life. Please be honest and very serious about it; it is not for anyone else's benefit but your own.

Let us talk about some powerful people of the past, people who possessed a great amount of faith. These people lived with a tremendous amount of success, prosperity, and happiness, because of the faith that they had in their God and in themselves. They didn't fail; they succeeded.

Let's start with the man, Abraham. He was a very faithful man to his God. He believed in his God enough that he was in the stage of knowing Him. Abraham knew that God was on his side, and he knew what God could and would do for him. So he let God control his life, because he knew that there couldn't be any mistakes in his life if he let God control it for him. When God told Abraham that He was going to have a son with his wife, Sarah, well, at first they both laughed. God repeated Himself to him, and then Abraham knew that He wasn't just joking. He was serious about it. (This story you would find in the book of Genesis, chapter 18.) He believed what his God had said to him, and that was because he knew that his God was the true God and that He made no mistakes. Therefore, he knew that he was going to have a son with his wife. Abraham didn't only *believe* but, most importantly, he *knew* that he was going to have a son with his wife, even though they were already old. But because his God said so and he knew because he had the faith that he needed to let it happen, it just had to happen, and it did happen. It happened not just because he believed, but because he knew, and because he had the proper faith,

Abraham had a tremendous amount of faith in his God. He was so close to Him that his God would speak to Abraham who would have conversations with Him. God would answer Abraham.

Now, can you just imagine talking to God and having Him talk back to you?

How wonderful that would be! Can you realize that if you were this close to God, you could get everything you needed or wanted? You would experience all the success you could handle, and more. Witness how successful and prosperous Abraham was because of the amount of faith that he had in God.

Well, after Abraham's son was a little older but still a very young child, God told Abraham that he had to sacrifice his son. Sacrifice meant to kill him and burning him as a burnt offering. Because Abraham knew his God so well and he had such faith in Him, even though he loved his son so much, he listened and obeyed his God's command. He obeyed because he knew that there was a true reason for this command. But because Abraham proved to his God that he really had true faith in Him, at the last moment, God spared his son and gave him a lamb to burn as an offering instead. This you will find in chapter 22 of Genesis.

Well, can you just imagine how happy Abraham must have been? He was probably the happiest man in the whole world. His faith in his God grew stronger and stronger, and he would never say no to Him. It didn't matter what the command was, Abraham always knew that there had to be a very good reason for it, or God wouldn't give him such command.

Because of the true faith that Abraham had in Him, he had a long, happy, and successful life. He is well known to this day as one of the most faithful and successful men who ever lived.

Now, if you just think for a moment, Abraham had enough faith to obey such command, but if he had lacked true faith in his God, or if he hadn't known Him as he did, he probably would have said, "get thee behind me, Satan" just as Jesus said in Matthew 4: 10. When He was tempted by Satan. Humanly speaking, Abraham would have thought that Satan was talking to him and trying to destroy his happiness and his family. But, no, Abraham knew very well that it was his God talking to him, and there was no mistaking it. His faith brought him prosperity, wealth, success, and happiness in his life. God kept his promise to Abraham and gave him nation after nation with so many descendants that it was impossible to count them all; they became like the stars in the sky or like the sand on the beach. Genesis 22: 17.

Now, we have to realize the difference between someone who has true faith and someone else who doesn't truly understand what real faith is and what faith can do. Faith makes miracles possible. For a man like Abraham, who thought that he and his wife would never have any children because they were old, faith made fatherhood possible.

So a man who wouldn't of had any descendants whatsoever, because he and his wife thought that they both were already too old to have any children, became a father. Because of his faith in his God, he became the great Father of many nations, because his God kept His promise to him. He had promised all of that to Abraham, and He provided. He did much for him because He loved Abraham as His son, and Abraham loved his God also as his Father.

Because He had true faith in His God, He received from Him all that he wanted and needed, and much more. He received more than he could even have dreamed possible.

Now, I would like you to stop reading for a while and concentrate on what you have already read. Make sure that you properly understand what you've read before you read any further.

Please stop now.

Now let us speak off another man of great faith. This man is far too important to leave behind or ignore. His name was Moses. I believe that Moses was probably the most faithful man who ever lived on Earth, next to our brother, Jesus Christ.

Moses was enlightened by God. I believe it is safe to say that, after his enlightenment, Moses did not know any limitation. God gave him dominion over all, and Moses knew it very well. He didn't let anything get in his way to stop Him from doing what he was supposed to do. Like Abraham, when God gave Moses a command, he obeyed it without hesitation whatsoever and without any reason whatsoever. If there would have been any hesitation, it wouldn't have been because he didn't believe enough in his God, because he not only believed, but he also knew ahead of time that anything that he would set himself to do in the favor of God, He knew that it would certainly be done even before he even started. He knew that with the faith that he had, there was no limitation in whatever he wanted to do. But Moses also knew that it had to be for the good of God's people, all his brothers and sisters. With the wisdom and faith that he possessed, nothing could stop him, and nothing was impossible to him.

We have to realize that it took a fair amount of faith just to open up a pathway through the sea for God's people to walk through, and then let the waters close up again after the people were freed, safe from the Egyptians, and on their way to the Promised Land. God let him know what to do and what he could do, and Moses knew there was no mistaking the knowledge that he was getting from God. Therefore, he was always willing and ready to obey God whenever He spoke to him. Moses knew very well that it was all for the betterment of all His people. He was on God's side, and he knew that God was also on their side every step of the way.

Because Moses had such a tremendous amount of faith, and because he was so obedient to his God and knew no limitations, some of us believe that Moses was taken up by God, without experiencing an ugly physical death, as we see it. While he was still on Earth and among his people, you would find throughout the book of Exodus all the miracles Moses performed, for there were many.

We realize that there have been many others who had tremendous amounts of faith. As we know, they are called saints because of their faith. They certainly deserve to be called saints, because some of them even died to keep their faith in their God, rather than to follow the evil path.

Their faith was so strong that they didn't only believe, but also they really knew the truth about the reality of life. They wouldn't just give it up, for any reason.

As I have said before, faith is one of the most powerful gifts and tools we could ever have and use to become powerful and successful in our physical and spiritual lives. We must realize that faith is not just believing that God can and will do everything for you, but real and true faith is also believing strongly enough to know that you can do anything you wish to do and have anything you wish to have, if only you have the faith and the will to do so. We must realize that God already has given all of us everything we need to succeed and prosper in our lives. We have to remember, as I've said before, that God gave us dominion over all. (This you can find in the first chapter of Genesis.) Remember, too, that Jesus said if we have faith, everything is possible and nothing is impossible to us. (This you will find in the book of Matthew.) We should study these passages from the Bible, get the proper understanding, and realize that it is the truth, and nothing but the truth, and that it is the true reality in our lives.

Believe in God, believe in yourself, believe the teachings of Jesus, especially The Sermon on the Mount, and The Beatitudes. I believe The Beatitudes are one of the most powerful readings of the Bible. Read it again and again until you understand it properly. Please don't think that you understand it enough and go on reading further, because we know that we can read through the whole Bible and think we know the Bible. But if you don't understand the true message, then you don't know the Bible or understand it as you really should; So, I have to say, please don't think that you know the whole Bible because you have read it once and understood a few passages. After reading it once, you probably get an idea of what it is about, but let me tell you that, at that point, you have barely started. We may have a quick view of the whole picture, but we don't really have the proper understanding of the whole message. We haven't studied the Bible enough to be able to put all of the puzzle pieces together the proper way, so that we could see and understand the whole picture, as we really should. Our goal should be to know what it is meant to be realized and understood by everyone, and there is no exception whatsoever.

Reading the Bible is one thing, but that isn't all. The main part is to study it and come to understand it the way it should be understood. Then and only then can we say that we understand what the Bible is really saying to us and what it means.

When we really get to understand what the Bible is about, then we can start using it for its purpose in our life. It is not so hard to do, because all you have to do at the beginning is just keep what you study in mind, as much as you can, think about what you've learned from it, and start putting it into practice, even just a little each day. Before you know it, you start realizing that you are growing spiritually, and that's when you start feeling stronger and happier. Then you know that there is success and prosperity ahead. You also start developing faith in yourself, as well as in God, and as Jesus said, in Matthew 17: 20. With faith, nothing is impossible to us. So, the proper route to take is to read and study the Bible very carefully; make certain that you do understand it properly. When you do, you can say that you know the word of God, and obey it.

We know that if anyone tries to get away without gaining a true understanding of the message, then this person just won't really get anywhere in life. People could be just fooling themselves just by thinking that they know the Bible after reading it once or twice, but they really don't understand it as well as it should be understood. Therefore, people can get fooled very easily by thinking that they understand the Bible enough to live according to its messages and its meanings. It is a matter of fact that when people read the Bible for the first time and get some understanding of it they get very happy and excited. They feel blessed; they feel that there is faith developing inside, and there is power in it. It is certainly something to be very happy and excited about, but it doesn't stop there. It's just the beginning. So, people shouldn't believe that they understand the Bible enough to be happy for the rest of their lives just from what was read once or twice. Remember that there is always more understanding to come with more practice.

Studying the Bible and getting to understand it properly is

how we understand the reality of life. When we realize what the reality of life really is, and we live our life the way it was meant to be lived, then there is no reason for any suffering to enter into our lives and prevent our happiness. Suffering is an ugly end in itself in life. There is no future in it because suffering is an ugly, evil thing that we certainly don't need. But true love, true faith, and true happiness mean success and prosperity in life.

Please don't make the mistake of thinking that you know and understand the Bible enough and stop reading or studying it. It is far too important in everyone's life. We must make an effort and study more, and the more we study, the more we understand the message. The more we study and practice, the more successful we grow in developing faith, which is so important for everyone. With the proper faith, we can get anything we want or need.

Faith is very powerful, and the more you study the word of God, the more you develop the proper understanding of it all. You start feeling more intelligent, and when you start feeling that way, and then you start feeling that there is a development of faith occurring inside of you. We know that with enough faith, nothing is impossible to us. So we have to remember and realize that if there are problems in our lives, they do not happen because God doesn't love us, tries to punish us, or doesn't want to take care of us anymore. If we have difficulty developing our faith within ourselves, it is only because of our own lack of understanding.

Lack of understanding usually is caused by our own refusal to listen, learn, and obey. That also means refusing to make a mental effort to learn more about ourselves, about the human race, and about the truth of the reality of life and its purpose. Therefore, lack of understanding, refusal to make a mental effort to learn, prevents us from becoming intelligent, and growing wiser, as we've talked about in the previous chapters, is also caused by a lack of discipline. Let's be honest with ourselves; we all know that lack of discipline is also caused by our own mental laziness. So many people seem to think that it is the easy way out. But the truth is, it is the hard way out. A person would struggle an entire lifetime, and it would be because of lack of mental development and lack of understanding.

As I've said before, the problem is not with or from God, because we should realize that with God, there is no problem. The problems are with us. It is because we are a stubborn and weak nation, and we refuse to obey the message of God. The message of God is to have faith in God and faith in yourself. Having enough faith to know that there is a God is one thing, and most of us already know that. But having true faith in God and in oneself, as God has in his plan for us according to his teachings, and studying and obeying is something totally different for some people.

First of all, we have to be honest with ourselves and admit, at least to ourselves, that we are weak and that we all have a certain amount of mental laziness. If we want to succeed and prosper in life, then we have to work on this mental laziness. We have to realize it, make mental efforts, and practice those efforts in doing some integrated thinking. We must learn to listen and obey, which is for our own benefit. When we can do that, then we can start feeling stronger and happier. Then we can start getting the feeling of success and prosperity within ourselves, and the ability to have faith or to develop the power of faith within, as you may wish to put it.

Faith is a power, an ability, a gift, a blessing, a tool. It is something that everyone needs in their lives; it is a must have to succeed and prosper in everyone's life. There is no exception for anyone. It is a must for everyone equally, and without a thought otherwise; therefore, we have to do whatever is necessary to obtain this great power and ability, no matter the cost, no matter the mental efforts. It is worth everything and all the efforts and practices that we can put into it, because it is a blessing. Everyone needs many blessings in life to grow, physically and spiritually. There is no exception for anyone.

Anyone can think that he or she is intelligent, but it is not always the real truth. It is very easy for anyone to fool oneself. It can happen to anyone without even realizing it. I have seen it time and time again, by many different people.

Therefore, someone who is intelligent is a person who is willing to listen, learn, and obey, and who is not trying to change the truth just to make life easier. It just doesn't work; one would only be fooling oneself.

Jesus warned us of these kinds of mistakes; therefore, we should pay attention to His teachings, and listen, learn, and obey.

We know that it is easier to walk on the wrong path than it is to walk on the right path. I have to say that it might be easier at the time of the walk, but it doesn't last forever. But if you use common sense with faith, you will know that it is much more profitable to walk on the right path; it is where one can find true rewards, for there are no rewards to be found anywhere else except on the right path. Mostly, everyone knows that, but again, it takes some mental effort, and D.T.C to earn the reward.

Faith, wisdom, intelligence, common sense, prosperity, success, health, wealth, and happiness will be found on the right path. Nothing good can be found on the wrong path; it only offers disasters and struggles.

There is work to be done with the great tools mentioned in the previous chapters, including D.T.C.

I would like you to stop reading for a while, do some thinking, and concentrate on what you've read until now. Please make sure that you do properly understand what you've read before you continue any further. It is much more profitable for you to go back, read it again, and study it properly. Be certain that you do understand it properly before reading any further. Don't just keep on reading without really understanding the message that it is trying to reveal to you. You won't be able to put all the puzzle pieces together, so that you can really see the picture by the time that you get at the end of this study.

Please stop now.

> If you believe enough to have the proper faith, you can get anything you want, at any time.

Now, keep this in mind, and just think about it as often as you can; with the proper faith or with enough faith, "nothing is impossible to you." Think about how faith could be achieved, and how you could make it happen. Well, you have to study until you can understand how it really works, and what it could and would do for you in your life. Use common sense, and it will strengthen your faith; therefore, do whatever you need to do to get this great power and ability or gift, if you will, that everyone so desperately needs to succeed and prosper in our physical and spiritual walk.

Then you can live in harmony with the world around you and with the whole society.

It is a very good idea to take a moment to thank the Good Lord for giving you the ability to read and understand what you study. Do this each time before you study this book and your Bible, and ask Him to bless you along the way in your studies.

Know that God has already blessed you with your efforts and good will, even before you ask. Just let all of His blessings come down on you, and let it be done. Amen.

Review: Chapter 8, Faith

Faith is my favorite word next to love, and in my view, it is also the most powerful word next to love.

In this chapter, we've talked about how much power there is in faith, and how much power we can have if we have faith. As Jesus taught us, if we have faith even the size of a mustard seed, we can do all the work that He did and even greater works.

We say that to have faith is to believe without seeing, but I like to add to this statement: I believe that real true faith isn't only believing but knowing, because knowing without seeing in my view is stronger than believing without seeing.

We've talked about Abraham, a very faithful man who didn't need to see to believe when God spoke to Him. He didn't only believe that it was God talking to Him, He absolutely knew that it was God talking to Him. When God told Him to burn his only son, whom He loved so much, He knew that there wasn't any mistake. It was God speaking to Him, and he wasn't about to refuse any of his God's commandments for any reason whatsoever.

Because his faith was so strong, God kept His promise to Abraham and made him one of the greatest men who ever lived. He gave Him possessions that were almost unthinkable. Even though Abraham and his wife were old, God still gave them lots of descendents that even made nations after nations. Abraham and his wife were filled with God's glories, and Abraham was always known as the man of faith, and certainly for a very good reason.

We also talked about another very faithful man, and this man was Moses. I always like to refer to Him as "the man of God," even though there have been many men of God and still are. But this man, I find a little different, probably because of the works He did for God's people to free them from Egypt and lead them to the Promised Land, as God had promised them if they were faithful to Him and remained this way. Moses also had to have a very great amount of faith, because when He opened the sea, He already knew ahead of time that this very thing was going to happen. Even if God had already told Him what would happen ahead of time, which He probably did, Moses still needed a great deal of faith to know ahead of time that this was going to happen. I believe that it would be difficult to have stronger faith than this, and again, his faith made Him very great in the eyes of God.

As Jesus said, with the proper faith, nothing is impossible to us. There is no limitation to a faithful person. Jesus said it, and that's good enough for me.

Chapter 9

Common Sense

Common sense is a very major piece of the puzzle that shouldn't be over looked, ignored, or forgotten by anyone at any time in our lives.

A realization must take place, a realization that must be taken very seriously by everyone at all times with no exceptions. The true fact is, as I mentioned in Chapter 1, that we are all part of each other and all in the same family. Whether we accept this fact or not doesn't change the truth of it, because it is the real truth. It is the reality of life.

Therefore, anyone who has enough common- sense does realize that God is our Father, the Father of all creation, and that we are all brothers and sisters and all in the same family of God. Whether we realize this fact or not, the truth still remains that if one of us is hurting for any reason, we are all hurting in one way or another. Whether we do realize or not what is happening and why it is happening, or whether we want to believe the truth or not about the reality of life, doesn't change anything whatsoever in anyone's life. It is a universal law; therefore, in this life, we certainly need common sense. If anyone has any problem with this idea, then I suggest that this person start working on developing common sense, which is a practical understanding, or a mental ability or capacity. In other words, having common sense is having a mental ability to detect whether something is true or false, good or bad, right or wrong, and to be able to make the proper decision for the right reason and at the proper time. Therefore, any person with enough common sense should be able to judge things, actions, or time for themselves, without having anyone else judging or making decisions for them all the time. Having someone else do those kinds of things or actions for us all the time, or at any time, doesn't make us any smarter, it just makes us weaker while the others look smarter. When we get in that stage in our mind, then we become dependent on others and others don't see us as being very smart at all. The truth is that it should be the other way around, but it is all up to each of us for our own good and our own benefit.

When we become dependent on others for everything, it is either because someone is very ill or physically disabled, or only because we have become mentally lazy. Anyone who is mentally lazy is simply someone who doesn't have enough common sense, whether this person never had it or had it but lost it because of getting used to having others make decisions for them, and do everything for them. In the process, this person becomes spoiled, as we call it, which is also becoming mentally lazy, without realizing that they are down-grading themselves, physically, mentally, and spiritually. They are just fooling themselves by thinking that they are good enough or smart enough, that they can even have someone else doing everything for them; they really think that they are doing well for themselves, but they are just hurting themselves more than they realize.

It is certainly good to help others anytime someone is in need of our help, but we have to be able to realize that there is a problem and detect that problem when a person is becoming too dependent on us. We should be truthful enough to approach this person in a proper manner and have a talk with this person about this problem that we believe is occurring in his or her life. This would be having enough common sense to realize and detect the problem, and also having enough common sense to realize that it is caring enough to share this kind of love with this person. Anyone who is capable of doing such good deeds for anyone else has developed the proper understanding and enough common sense. This person is certain to have happiness and success in his or her life.

If we just stop for a moment and think about it, we realize that when we think good thoughts about someone else, we automatically feel good inside, but if we think bad thoughts about someone else, then after a while, we don't feel very happy for some reason. We really do feel as if something is wrong, things are not going right, and our emotions are not positive ones. Well, the true fact is that we have just hurt someone else, and we have hurt ourselves also in the process, without realizing what we've done by thinking negatively about a brother or a sister. That certainly should never happen. That is the feeling that we get from doing such things about others; as the Bible says, we reap what we sow.

Now whether we realize this fact or believe it, it doesn't change the fact that it is the truth. It is God's universal system and law, and there is absolutely nothing that we can do about it, except realize it, accept it, and obey it. We can be certain that things will go right in our lives. Remember: listen, learn, and obey is the key to happiness, success, and prosperity.

We should have enough common sense to understand that if we are obedient to God and His universal law, we certainly can't go wrong.

Therefore, if someone thinks or speaks wrongly about someone else, you can be certain that shortly afterward, things are not going to go as well, not as well as if there had been good, positive thoughts and spoken words about this person. If you find it hard to believe this fact, then all you have to do is check it out for yourself. Try it; it's very easy to do. Just keep the idea of positive thinking in your mind for one day, then go and visit someone. Spend your visit speaking good and positive thoughts about someone else; just pick the person that you want to talk about and make it a joyful visit. You will realize when it's time to leave that the person you were visiting was happy and enjoyed your visit. You will be going home happy, and you left the one you have visited happy also. Shortly after this, you will realize that because you've done a good deed, things seem to go much better and you are happier with yourself for what you've done. That is just the way it is. This is the reality of life in action, and whoever does the acting is rewarded openly by God our Father, which is in heaven. He is just waiting for us to take these kinds of actions, so that He can reward us openly with no hesitation whatsoever.

God knows our intentions even before we act; therefore, He has our reward ready for us even before we act. God loves to give to those who love to give. He loves to share his love with all his children equally, and He doesn't want to leave anyone behind. He doesn't like for any of us to stay behind and go astray.

Anyone with some common sense does realize that what we've just talked about is the truth and nothing but the truth. We also know that the teaching of the Bible says that we reap what we sow; therefore, we must take this idea very seriously if we want happiness and success in our life.

Remember that once we know the truth about the reality of life, there are no excuses for failure with our actions against our brothers and sisters. This means that we should be good and loving to everyone, all humanity and also all the great creations all of the time, because that was all created for our own benefit and success.

It is the great universal law, and no one has the ability to change it or any part of it. Therefore, it is very simple: either we obey the law or we fail.

We will have additional reading and study about the topic "obey the law or fail" later on, but for now, let's not fall off the subject. It is far too important to just skip it.

Now, I think that you probably should stop reading for a while. Review what you've just read, and study it properly. Make sure that you understand the passage properly before you read any further. Please take your time and be honest about it. I truly want you to understand the whole passage properly.

Please stop now.

⸺

Now, I would like to give you a true example concerning love, patience, common sense, self-respect, respect for others, dignity, and so forth.

Allow me to share with you, to the best of my knowledge, some experiences from my own life, starting from a very young age.

Coming from a large family of twelve children, the family started in the late 1920s and the last babies came in the early part of the 1950s. During those years, there wasn't much help coming from anyone but just our own family. There wasn't any welfare or any aid as people receive today, and times were so very hard sometimes. Well, it is true to say that we were very, very poor financially. The family started out on the right foot, as we say, on a farm, and there was always a lot of food for everyone to eat. The older ones started helping out on the farm at a very young age, as it was the fashion those days, but then, coming around the year that I was born or a few years before, since I was the tenth child, things started going the wrong way for the family. Things got harder and harder, and we got poorer and poorer. Some members of the family got very ill, and father had to sell some animals to pay for the doctors. Then, more illness, more doctors, and selling more animals to the point that there were no more animals to sell. The family was ruined and in trouble. We had real problems, and we had trouble just surviving.

Father had to look elsewhere for work, and since he didn't have the proper transportation to go to and from work, father decided to move the family closer to where he was working. But that job didn't last very long, and Father was still looking for work somewhere else, anywhere. But during all this time, the family was struggling to survive. When father would find a job, even if it only lasted for a short time, there was hope and there was some happiness in the family while that lasted. But there was struggle after struggle to survive for as long as I can remember, until all the children were gone on their own.

But even though we were so very financially poor, during that time of poverty, speaking for myself, I was so preoccupied worrying about food and about the next day and so forth, that my mind was only focused on negative thinking. Why are we so poor? Why did my parents have so many children? I wondered why father couldn't get a good, steady job like some other men, and so on. My mind was full of worries, struggles, and wonders about survival.

When I got older, I asked my father why they had so many children.

His answer was, "the more children you have, the more you love them." Well, I have to admit that his answer made me think for a while. He also said, "We have been very poor, and I know that you don't understand how or why, but let it be a teaching to you. I taught you things that you will find very useful later on in your life, and when that time comes, I know that you will understand. You will be fortunate to be able to use this teaching in your future, because it will help you a great deal, probably more than you think right now. I thought that he was just trying to make me feel better about everything, or that maybe he felt sorry about it and that he was just trying to cover up, or whatever. But I also thought that maybe he was right, maybe that's just the way it is, "The more children we have the more we love them." Still, I kept on thinking, *if it is true about this love thing for the children, then why bring more into this world to suffer?* But I remembered my father saying, "You don't understand now, but you will later on in your life." Just those words were enough for me to let it be as it was until I got old enough and experienced enough to really understand. But I was always anxious to get to this understanding and one day I surely did.

Unfortunately, my father died shortly after all the children were gone from home and on their own. He died from cancer at the age of sixty-five. He didn't even have the chance to see his first old age pension check.

But, it wasn't until my father passed away that I started realizing and understanding his teaching, and what he meant when he said, "I taught you things that you will be fortunate to have and use in your future, if you remember what I am telling you."

There was so much that my father thought us about so many things, just to get us prepared for our future. It seems as if that was the focus in his life, just to get us prepared for the future.

Let me give you an example of the things that he used to tell us. He would say, "Do you remember how things were going in your life about five years ago?"

Take a good look at the way the world is going now. Can you see a difference in five years?

If you remember this suggestion five years from now, take a good look at how things will be going, then compare the difference in those five years. Imagine how it is going to be in the next five years, ten years, twenty years, and so on. You should be able to prepare yourself for those years to come, without having too much difficulty adapting to the changes that you will be facing. That shouldn't come as too much of a surprise to you, when you will be living in those years, father would say. Things are changing so fast, and people are becoming so smart that it will be difficult just to keep up with the rest of the world. So try to understand to have as much common sense as possible, and it will not be too difficult for you to keep up with the rest of the world.

My father knew what common sense was all about and how important it was to have or to develop common sense. He had no education to speak of, but he was no fool either.

Still, when I was a child, we were so very poor financially, but we had riches that, at that time, I for one didn't realize that we had. I came to realize that even though we were financially poor, my father was very strong on teaching us about love for each other, respect for others, and dignity. He was very strong on teaching us about common sense, but I used to think that my father was hard on us, because he would make us listen to what he was saying to us. Now that I understand, though, I know that it was just because he loved us that much. He didn't have any money to send us to any special school, and he didn't have any education to speak of, but he had love for his children, and he wanted the best for us in our future.

His teaching was the best that he could offer to help to get us prepared for our future. I, for one, will be the first one to admit that he was good at it. I know that his teaching to me is probably one of the biggest reasons why I am writing this book, with true love and hope that it will help many readers for many years to come. Remember that because I have developed common sense, I got to realize and understand my father's teaching, and it helps me help others in many different ways. Because of the love that my father had and shared with us, I can share true love with you also. I have God to thank for giving me a father that loved and taught me the way that he did.

I can't forget to tell you that my father always made sure that we as children always went to church every Sunday morning; because he believed that we could learn more about God the Father and his son, Jesus, than what he could teach us about them. That was a start for us, and he truly believed that it would be more beneficial to us to attend church every Sunday, and listen and learn from the priest. But because we didn't really understand, we thought that Father was just being hard on us children, without realizing that he was using disciplinary actions on us for our own benefit. But all these efforts that he used on us now pay off for me. I have my father to thank for the efforts and the knowledge that he has implanted in me, even when I was too young to know. But now I do realize the meaning of his teaching, and that it is so helpful to me. I respect my father so very much for what he has done for me, all the efforts, the dedication, the patience that he had to just take the time to talk to us and teach us about what he understood about life.

As I've mentioned before, my father wasn't educated, but he certainly had a brain in his head and he was determined to use it on us at all costs. He believed that it would be easier for us after we went out on our own, and I appreciate him very much for his efforts that he dedicated for all his children. It couldn't be forgotten.

Father used to say, if you have good common sense, you won't have to worry. He would often say, don't get angry for nothing and have patience, and then you'll go a long way in life.

He was absolutely right. I now realize that there are so many things that we say and do that are lacking in any value whatsoever, just because we don't have or use enough common sense in our everyday life, in everything we say and do. That is the reason why there are so many problems today and so much struggle that we have to deal with every day of our lives. People make too many mistakes, just for the lack of good common sense and patience.

Common sense is a very big piece of the puzzle that must be put in its proper place. It is part of the reality of life; therefore, it is very well needed by everyone in our lives to find success. Anyone who uses common sense is a wise person.

Now I would like you to stop reading for a while and

concentrate on what you've read up until now. Make certain that you understand what you've read before you read any further. Make sure that you grasp the proper understanding of the whole picture before you read any further, so that you can visualize the picture that you have put together until now. If it is too difficult for you to grasp the proper understanding of it, and you can't see the real picture or even part of the picture, then I strongly suggest that you go back to the beginning of the chapter, and read it again and again until you properly understand it. It won't be as profitable to you if you don't, and again, I have to say that if you cannot do that, then that only means that you have a difficulty with your own common sense development. That means that you need to work on it and practice it as much as you can until you have it right and have this problem conquered. It will make it much easier for you to understand the remainder of the book, so please don't be in a hurry to read any further unless you understand all the passages properly. You will find the remainder of the book much easier to follow, so please be patient with me, and follow these instructions. In the end, you will be happy that you did.

Please stop now.

If you have common sense, then you know how beautiful you are on the inside

Review: Chapter 9, Common Sense

This is one of my favorite topics, because I know that without common sense, we can't do much that's worth doing. Everyone needs common sense to get anywhere in life, to reach a goal, to succeed and prosper in any way. People who can't use or develop common sense, unfortunately, are unable to become very smart or intelligent among their peers. They will fall behind and struggle to get anything done that is worth doing. Therefore, common sense is a very strong tool that all of us really need to use to control our lives the proper way. Someone who can use or develop common sense is a person who usually would learn things very easily and quickly compared to someone else that has difficulty using common sense with anything they do or anything that they try to learn. Because that makes it so much more difficult for them to learn anything, they have to go through life struggling. Nevertheless, I believe that this tool can be taught to almost anyone, anyone who is willing to listen and learn.

As I've mentioned in this chapter, my father wasn't very well educated. In fact, he didn't have any education at all to speak of. But when it came to common sense, he certainly was there to straighten us out, and very quickly at that. He just couldn't stand to see anyone doing anything that didn't make sense to him. He would get frustrated and sure would let us know what he thought of us for doing something of the sort.

We must remember that to become smart or intelligent,

we need to have or develop common sense, or stay behind the others.

Chapter 10

Patience

Patience is another very important piece of the puzzle that should be recognized, because it is much more important than people realize.

As we very well know, or should know, patience is a virtue. Now, if we know what virtue really is or what it really means, then we know how important patience really is. We should all practice and work with this very powerful tool in our lives.

Virtue is a very powerful tool that can take you a long way in life. It takes a wise person to understand, practice, and use this power appropriately. A person who is able to use this ability at all times is a person who has very good qualities and uses these qualities in life for the right reasons. Someone who uses patience all the time is the kind of person who emanates goodness and the power of love. When we talk with such people, we want to talk with them more, because we feel so good. We can't help but feel their gentleness, and most of the time, these people don't even realize how good they make us feel while we are talking to them. We are happy to have found a new friend. Most of the time, we don't take time to stop and think about why we feel good about talking to this person. We simply like this person, but we don't really know the real reason why we feel this way.

Some people have very good qualities and use those qualities in their lives all of the time. People really like them because of their love and the kindness that they share with others. Sometimes, it is also a very good teaching to others, as we know actions speak louder than words. People exhibiting kindness can be a very great help to others, who would see or recognize what makes these people the way they are and want to be like them. We can practice emulating kind and loving people, and after a while, we, too, would have people liking us and wanting to be our friends. Through practice, we would develop good qualities, and people would feel the same way about us now as they did with the others. People are attracted to us because of the love and kindness we have, and because we are willing to share it with anyone else.

As we discussed in previous chapters, we know very well that if we bring happiness into someone else's life, we are certain to be rewarded in one way or another. Having and sharing good qualities with someone else is doing God's will. It is pleasing to Him in a very high degree; therefore, it is very rewarding.

It is no secret that we all want to be rewarded for anything that we do, as long as whatever we do is done for the good of everyone. Even a good thought about someone else is very rewarding. We very well know that it is something very good to work on and practice. It is a very good quality that people should see in you and feel from you.

Most, if not all, of these great qualities could come from working with patience. Practice patience, and these qualities will develop in you just like magic. Let's face it, if patience is a virtue, and virtue is full of qualities, then patience must be a very powerful tool to use in our lives, wouldn't you say?

Let's talk a bit about a different kind of value that we find in patience. For example, if we were to ask God for something, should we expect to receive it immediately, or lose all faith because we didn't receive it immediately, or have enough patience and wait until we do receive it? Will our faith grow stronger because we have received?

I believe that sometimes God could be just testing our faith. If we prove that we really have faith in Him, then He will answer. If we have enough patience and prove our faith, then we can get a greater answer then we expected, and it is certainly worth the wait.

Don't get me wrong here with these words. Sometimes we do get an immediate answer from God, but for some reason, it's an answer only He can understand. We may not get our answer as quickly as we would like, but believe me, He knows why. You can be certain that He has a very good reason why sometimes it takes a while for Him to give us our answer. If you don't give up on Him and exercise the powerful quality of patience, without losing faith, He will answer you and you will certainly be very pleased with His answer.

This is very simple: with God, patience is very rewarding. In other words, if you are patient with Him, He will be patient with you, too. He will reward you openly, and the same goes for all of God's children. He wants everyone to be patient with each other as He is patient with all of us. If we can do that, He will reward us openly, because this is His word. He promised.

Therefore, if we practice patience and develop kind and loving qualities, then we are certain to have happiness and success in our lives. This isn't true only for a few or certain people; it is true for everyone. It doesn't matter our race, gender, or color, in the eyes of God, we are all equal. We are all brothers and sisters. We are all the children of the same God, and He loves us all equally.

Let me tell you a little story about myself concerning patience. Some years ago, I had decided to open a business. I really wanted this business to get started as soon as possible, and I could hardly wait. I was too anxious to get going with it, because this was something that I really love doing.

It seemed as if it was taking forever, and I couldn't get going soon enough for my liking. I was getting frustrated and sick and tired of waiting, so one day, I decided to talk to God about it and see if I could speed things up. I was applying for a loan with the federal government, and there was so much paperwork to be done, so many letters to write to the surrounding communities, and so many estimates to make up, and so forth. It seemed as if something was always getting in the way and causing a delay. I was getting tired of all this paperwork and all these delays. I was really getting frustrated with all of the bureaucracy.

Well, I thought, if I have a good talk with God and ask Him to fix this up for me and help me get this business going right away, then I'll be on my way. I'll be happy about it because I'll have what I really want. So I prayed, hoping that I would get a phone call very soon. But the next day came, and no phone call about this matter. Well, the next evening I prayed again, hoping to get a phone call the next day, but again, it didn't happen. And the same thing again the next day, and the day after, and after a while, with all my frustration, I sat in my office chair with my hands wrapped around my head, and started thinking really hard. I was thinking properly about this entire manner one step at the time.

Well, at first I thought the reason why nothing was happening was that I must have been doing something wrong. So, I decided to have a real serious talk with God about it. I still had the feeling that nothing was going to happen, so I thought, what in the world is wrong here? I knew that God couldn't be wrong; therefore, I must be still doing something wrong. I decided to ask God to show me what I was doing wrong, instead of just asking Him for what I wanted right away, like a selfish child.

Well, wouldn't you know, there was a small book on the far corner of my desk that I had bought before and never read yet. As soon as I asked God to show me what I was doing wrong, without even thinking about anything else, my eyes went straight to that book that was just sitting among other books and papers. To top it all off, it was the very bottom book that was sitting there. I could only see the edge of it, but my eyes were fixed on that book, and there was no leaving it there or forgetting about it, either. I felt as if a voice in my head was telling me that my answer was in that book. Then, just as if this voice was saying, "Don't just look at it, pick it up! Pick it up and open it." At first, I found that kind of weird, but I was curious, so I reached and picked up this small book of one to two hundred pages. I opened it up about a third of the way in, and the page just happened to be a teaching about patience and some other great tools. It only took me about two minutes to realize what my problem was. The book said if we really want good things to happen in our lives, we must understand what these tools are and how they work. I've past that book to someone else that needed this kind of help, and never seen it again, but I believe that the name of the book was: Answers to Prayers, by George Mueller. We must put these tools in place and work with them properly, and if we do work with them properly, then we develop faith. With the proper faith, everything is possible to us.

The great teaching of this short passage was that we have to work with these tools all together for them to work properly. It also said that there shouldn't be any tools missing. Patience was certainly one tool among the others, which we will be talking about later on.

My problem was lack of patience. I was certainly going to do something about it using the other tools. I would work with them starting right now, I said to myself. I am going to work with these tools the proper way. I already know that good things are going to happen now, and there is no doubt whatsoever about this. Almost miraculously, I received a message in my mind; it was like a ribbon with words on it waving through my mind. This message was just as clear as anything you could ever imagine. The message was this: at three o'clock tomorrow afternoon, you will get the phone call you have been waiting for. I walked out of my office to tell my wife what had happened. I said that the next afternoon, I had to be by the phone to receive my call. I'm not sure if she really believed it; she probably didn't know if she should believe it. Nevertheless, the next day before three o'clock, I was sitting by the phone, and I absolutely knew that this call was coming at exactly that time. To no surprise at all, at exactly three o'clock, the phone rang. I was told by my caseworker that everything went through, my loan had been approved and accepted, and I had to go to the city to sign some papers and receive the loan. Well, just like magic, but I call it a miracle, God had spoken to me. He answered me because I had proved my faith to Him, in a very positive way. I also call that an act of faith.

In any case, the point is, I realized what I was doing wrong, or what I wasn't doing that I should have been doing, and that what I was lacking was patience. See, I believed I had the faith I needed, as well as the hope, the will to let it happen, the desire to have it happen, enough wish to even dream about it happening, and the love to make things happen—but it still wasn't happening. I was missing a tool, and this tool was patience.

It was just as if there was a missing link in the chain; therefore, there was a power missing among the others. Therefore, there wasn't the full force working, because all of these tools must be working together to make things happen. I had learned my lesson. Coincidentally, I also had been working on using those tools, experiencing how they work and how powerful they really are, but my real experience then was that these tools must work together. At the same time, to have the full strength of the group of tools at work, they must be put in order and put to work simultaneously. Once everything is in place, we can just watch it happen. It works just like magic.

I would like you to stop reading for a while, and concentrate on what you've read until now. Study it properly so that you can understand all of it before you read any further.

Please take your time and be certain that you can put these puzzle pieces together, and at their proper places, so that you can see and understand what the whole picture looks like and what it means. Then you can start working with it and profiting from it.

Please stop now.

⏤

This certainly was a great teaching to me. Let's be sure we understand the message: one tool doesn't necessarily work as well as we would like it to work. Unless we combine it with the others, we won't be successful, even though we might think that we have the proper faith needed to make things happen, as Jesus said. If we don't have the power of love within us and use it properly, or patience, for example, as it is such powerful and important tool to use, then we simply don't have the proper faith or we don't allow it to work for us when we might need it the most.

As I mentioned in Chapter 2, we must work with D.T.C. We have to learn about these very important tools, what they really are and how they work, and then practice working with them. That is the only way to gain the proper faith, intelligence, and wisdom needed to make things happen for us. It is a universal law; it is the reality of life. Just recognizing this fact and living according to it, or even just practicing working with these tools, is already a very great advantage. We are working with God and his universal laws, and that is doing God's will. Everyone knows that when we are doing God's will, He will be on our side and He will make us successful. God made that promise to all his children, and He never changes His word.

God's word will last forever. It cannot be changed or twisted around at anytime just to suit us. It is a known fact that some people already have tried that and failed. Anyone who tries to change something so powerful is sure to fail in his or her life.

Now, going back to working with these tools, that may sound like a lot of work, but after trying it seriously for a while, it becomes easy. It does become a joyful thing to do, and it is very rewarding. We just have to remember that we have nothing to lose and everything to gain from it.

We must remember that, when we use these tools, we can't expect to receive good and strong results immediately. We shouldn't give up right away just because we didn't receive anything instantly. Remember that patience is a very powerful tool, and it must be put to work with the other tools to achieve success in our lives. We do have to understand that, with the proper faith, nothing is impossible to us. But we also have to realize that if we don't have enough patience, then faith just doesn't work the way we would like it to work. Without patience, faith is simply much too weak. Even though we may think that we have enough faith, if we were to have the power of faith within us, we would be just weakening our faith by the lack of patience. That isn't going the right way at all. It is being at a standstill, and we are really stopping anything from happening, or at least we are slowing down the process of anything important that we are trying to accomplish.

People who have patience usually have the faith needed to make things happen, especially when they understand what patience really is, how much power it has, and what it can do for them.

Unfortunately, because of a lack of knowledge or understanding about these facts, many people just give up. They quit trying because they get frustrated and lose faith. They go through life just struggling and suffering, sometimes struggling just to survive or make ends meet. They don't even know why or what to do about it, or how to get out of that ugly rut.

Sometimes, people can't develop the proper faith because of the way they were raised as a child. Maybe they are too used to getting their way with their parents, and they were getting everything they wanted. That would make it much more difficult for them to develop the proper patience, which a person cannot properly work with those tools. Therefore, nothing very good ever happens, and these people don't even know why. Even though they tried so hard to get what they needed, and they really don't understand why nothing is happening. They get frustrated and quit trying. They give up on faith; actually, they even lose faith in themselves. Most of the time, this loss of faith results from a lack of understanding about how powerful faith really is and how it works together with the other tools. People need to understand how powerful these tools are when they are combined; they do receive strength from each other. By practicing using combinations of tools, people can develop the proper faith. They can make things happen in their lives, and the more they see things happening, the stronger their faith gets.

When people have this kind of difficulty getting whatever they really need in their lives, and they get frustrated and give up on everything, they just go on living the same old way. Sometimes, people even give up on God or quit believing in God because it doesn't seem to matter what they do, or how much they pray, because nothing ever happens in their life.

All this time, they don't realize the fact that they need to stop trying for a moment and take a good hard look at themselves. When they recognize the fact that the problem is with their lack of understanding about how they really are, and what they really need to do about this problem that they have, they can change.

When they do this with an open mind and the proper honesty, being truthful at least with themselves, they will really understand that, as mentioned in the previous chapters, they need to work with D.T.C.

Once people realize what the problem really is, they must use disciplinary actions to change for the better. Then they can make things happen in their lives, and before they know it, they can see how wonderfully it works. It seems to work just like magic.

People realize that one of the biggest problems was probably their lack of patience, because they lacked an understanding about these powerful tools that are so very important in everyone's life to succeed and prosper.

It is very sad to see sometimes how so many people lose faith in themselves, and even in God, just because of a lack of understanding. Therefore, it is very important for anyone to get educated, by reading and studying different books, good and important books, especially the Bible. The Bible contains everything and everyone, and it explains all about its content and all about the truth about the reality of life.

We also know that it is very important to read and study other truthful books, like this very book for example, because sometimes, good books will bring someone to read the Bible and get a better understanding of it all. Understanding makes life much easier to handle. To act with a positive attitude toward life and find real happiness and success in it is worth all the effort that is put into it. Understanding is happiness, it is reality of life, and it is everything in people's lives.

Patience is much more important than people realize. Let me give you an example of it.

Let's say that a man loves his wife very much and he does admit that his wife is everything to him. However, this man doesn't have much patience with his wife, or even with anyone else around him, because he doesn't like to wait for her to get ready when they go somewhere, for example. Or, when he wants her to do something for him, and he doesn't really have the patience to wait for her to have things done for him, sometimes he gets frustrated because of it. He might even tell her off about it and can get pretty nasty with his wife at times. He doesn't realize how much he really hurts his wife with all these nasty words and with his nasty attitude. He even hurts others that just happen to be around him when he gets nasty.

But when he doesn't need his wife to do anything for him for a while, then he is nicer to her. He tells her how much he really loves her, how much she means to him, and how he really appreciates her, and so on. All's well until he again has to wait for her, then he becomes the same old grouch again. Just speaking for myself, I would call that ignorance and hypocrisy. If a man really truly loves his wife, he would find a way to be patient with her, and he would be willing and ready to help himself with his problems. He wouldn't simply use his wife as someone to release his frustrations on. That is not true love. The real reason why he cannot live without her is just because she is always there for him whenever he needs her.

Let's face it for real. Many times, what could be a great and lasting marriage doesn't last very long, because while he was taking advantage of her, she was getting sick and tired of being treated this way. Unfortunately, her love gradually is fading away, and all faith and hope that they once had for their future are getting lost. Finally, disaster strikes, and everything that they were hoping for, the great plans they had made for their future are dead and gone. They finally separate, and there is no coming back for anything that they shared.

We can't forget that, most of the time, there are children left to pay the price for someone else's wrongdoings, and that is always very sad to see.

Everyone suffers, and that could be just because one of the parents has a problem and refuses to admit it and to deal with it. It could be either the husband or the wife. Sometimes, the trouble could be from both of them, which is certainly no better at all in any case.

Lack of patience, and D.T.C., can destroy good marriages. Everything else that is worth having, mental strength, including happiness, becomes disastrous in people's lives.

Therefore, if both of them have patience, especially for each other, then there should be real love, and with real love for each other and their children, then the great reward is happiness and success. As I've said before, where there is happiness, there is success, and with that, there is prosperity. This is surely what reality of life is all about and there is no mistaking it.

We can't forget that when we are living this kind of life, we are really doing the will of God. This really pleases Him, because this is the kind of life God wants His children to live. That's when, from His storehouse, He pours out his blessings on His children and makes them prosper in every way possible. God is the Father of all, and therefore, He is the great leader of all. He holds the key to happiness. Ask and you shall receive, knock and it will be opened onto you, search and you shall find, as the Bible says.

Speaking for myself, I know that whenever I lack patience for a while, I don't feel well. Something is wrong. Before long, I do realize that I am doing something wrong, but what is it?

I just have to stop and think about it for a moment. It sure doesn't take me very long before I realize what it is that I am doing wrong, and it doesn't take me very long either to repair the damage. But as a human being like everyone else, sometimes it does take me a little longer than it should before I realize that there is a problem I need to work on, and that the problem is in and with me. No one else should be to blame for this problem;

neither should anyone else pay nor suffer because I have a problem. This is the reality of life that has to be looked at and taken very seriously.

There were some times in my life when things were not so easily dealt with, because I used to be stubborn and hot headed. I wasn't very easy to deal with, either, sometimes, because like lots of others, I didn't want to be wrong in the best of times. Maybe I just didn't want to see myself being wrong often, either, so I would rather sweep it under the rug, as we say. But somewhere down the road, something really went wrong. I truly found myself wrong and I couldn't just sweep it under the rug this time. I really had to deal with the truth, face to face, and with honesty.

I asked God to forgive me, and I've found a way to forgive myself. I knew that to be forgiven, I had to be able to forgive myself. That was the only way that I could build up strength in myself. As the Bible says in Matthew, chapter 6, "Forgive and you will be forgiven by our heavenly Father." Therefore, forgiveness played a big part in it for me.

I was able to find the strength and the understanding that I needed enough to be able to work on myself and correct my problems. It took lots of courage, dedication, determination and D.T.C., but I wasn't about to quit. I just kept on striving to heal and become a better person. I did this for myself and also for everyone else. I have to say that I never been so satisfied with anything else before, as I am with my success on this matter. It was so rewarding that I just kept on working on myself in any way I could. I did this work also so that someday I could help others resolve their problems as I did my own. When it came to learning more about myself, others, and the reality of life, I've become so interested. I found that it was such joy just to see myself getting better in such wonderful ways. The urge I always had to help others became a reality in my life, and that was a breakthrough for me. I knew then that my dream to help others was coming true, and I knew that I was reaching my goal. By now, after so many years, I have finally reached my goal. To me, it is my biggest reward for doing what I did, before I could reach out and help someone else in the way that I am doing now. It is such pleasure to be able to do this work, and I wouldn't change this for anything else.

Understand here that the truth is that I had a goal to reach. I was determined enough to do whatever was necessary to reach my goal. First of all, I asked our heavenly Father to be by my side at all times and help me with my efforts in becoming a better person. I promised to be patient about it, and I knew that the more work I would put into it, the sooner I would reach my goal. I very well knew that with God on my side, I couldn't go wrong. I also knew that with Him on my side, it would be easier for me to conquer my problems and to become the person that I had wanted to be for such a long time.

At first, I have to admit that I didn't know how to use all of these tools, how they worked, and how long it would take before I would see some results from my efforts. All the intense mental work and hard integrated thinking was helpful, as was doing some disciplinary actions on myself and D.T.C. But one thing I knew that really helped me was the fact that I couldn't fail as long as I had God on my side. I also knew that I couldn't fail and I would reach my goal because what I was doing would benefit others when I could help anyone who needed my help. We know that when someone is helping others this way, then this person just cannot fail. The help is given with patience and with the power of love, and love never fails. Love can never fail because it is God's promise and His universal law. Love could never be changed, it is forever lasting.

Now I can say that I really feel good about myself and with my God for helping me through all these years. I'm proud about my efforts and studies to become a better person and to become successful in reaching my goal.

Well, you know what they say; God helps those who help themselves. In this case, there is certainly no mistaking it. It was proven to me again, and when someone sees this kind of thing happening and experiences it, that is when all doubts disappear. You feel yourself getting the power to conquer any negative that may come your way, and I'll tell you that this kind of feeling would be very difficult to ignore.

The real truth is, if you believe in yourself, have faith in God, and trust in Him, you will not fail. Happiness, success, and prosperity are at hand. Amen.

Now I would like you to stop reading again for a while, and truly concentrate on what you've read until now. Please make sure that you truly understand all that you've read right from the very beginning before you read any further.

In any case, I truly believe that it would benefit you probably more than you think if you did go back and read it again from the very beginning. If you did, then I know that you would be very happy that you did, especially because of what you would grasp that you might have been missed before now. It does happen all the time, so don't feel bad about it; if you've missed anything before, just be happy that you've got it now. But that is if you are patient enough to go back and read it again, right from the beginning. Remember that it is for no one else's benefit but your own.

Please stop now.

May God help and bless you with your studies.

If you have patience like I've asked you to have, then you will succeed with your studies

Review: Chapter 10, Patience

Well, we very well know that if we don't have patience, we are very hard to get along with, and if we are hard to get along with, then that only means that we are not very likeable or loveable. Therefore, we would think that it must be a miserable way of living, and just to know that we are difficult to deal with, I don't believe that a person could really be happy with himself or herself. Therefore, why not doing something about changing their ways or their habits or whatever deeds to be done, to make themselves a better person to cope with or to live with, so that they too could be happy with everyone else.

Lack of patience can cause disasters in a family. It can break what could be a very beautiful and happy marriage, but because of lack of patience, it is nothing but disaster for the whole family.

This also goes for the people that we have to work with every day. We put up with their grumblings all day because we know that a person without patience cannot be happy. Working with someone who's hardly ever happy isn't pleasant for anyone, either. The pure truth is that it is a very hateful day at work with someone like that. We should certainly do something about it. We can't forget that it isn't as safe as it would be if everyone were happy working together.

This isn't something new. We see this all the time on any job site. Patience is a virtue, which I believe it should be practiced and lived accordingly.

Chapter 11

Forgiveness

How powerful this word really is. We might say that forgiveness is the key to open heaven's door to meet our Lord at the judgment day.

It is unfortunate that there are so many people who do not understand the true meaning of this powerful word.

If only people would visualize and realize how many great blessings a person can receive from being able to truly forgive someone else, to realize how wonderful it will be to meet our Lord face to face, with real joy and happiness, and receive salvation, everlasting life, given to us by God Himself.

I really don't think that there could be any joy and happiness greater then to be called the true son or daughter of God, and live with Him for eternity.

We have to realize that Jesus very well knew what He was saying, when He said, it is easier for a camel to go through the eye of a needle than it is for a man to enter the kingdom of heaven. Well, humanly speaking, it was a very true statement. This is a very good example of what He said, because He very well knew how difficult it is for so many people to truly forgive others their trespasses. Forgiveness is especially difficult when someone has harmed us; someone that may have said something that really hurt our feelings or may have robbed us of anything we own. In an extreme case, someone that may have murdered a loved one, tried to murder us, or threatened to do so.

We know that it is much easier said than done, but the truth is that it is much more beneficial to do the actual forgiving than to just want to do it or just think about doing it.

Some people may think that they've forgiven someone else because they said that they did. But, some time later, they still feel bad or still hurt from it. Well, in this case, the actual forgiving never took place. Sometimes people will realize that they do have to forgive to be forgiven, so they will say that they have forgiven the other, because their wish is to be forgiven, but in reality, they don't really want to forgive the other or just can't find the strength to do it.

Sometimes lack of forgiveness can be because a person just doesn't know how to forgive; really forgive, because true forgiveness can only be achieved if it is done from the heart, mind, and soul. Only then is it and truly active. It is a true fact that not everyone can really forgive.

The reason why not everyone can actually forgive is because some people never knew how. They were never taught and never understood the true meaning of forgiveness and how important it really is. Consequently, some people really think that they have forgiven someone else just because they said that they did, but the truth is, at the end, there wasn't any actual forgiving. Many think that they should receive great results from their forgiveness to others.

Many people can get fooled with this kind of thing, just because they don't know any better and don't know how to do it properly.

We have to realize that people who don't really know how

to truly forgive can't really forgive themselves, either. It is really sad to know that so many people in this world are living in such situations, in other words, living with this kind of lack of understanding, Understanding is so important in everyone's life.

True forgiveness can only be done with the heart, mind, and soul if the power of love is in action. Without the power of love, nothing good happens. It is reality, and it is God's universal law that could never be changed. Therefore, it has to be taken very seriously and obeyed by everyone.

It is very important for everyone to study and learn about the real meaning of the word, the real power that it holds, and what tools we should use to be successful with it. The power of love is certainly the main one.

If, for any reason, you have difficulty with these tools, either in knowing how they work or how to use them then, I strongly suggest that you go back to the love chapter and read it and really study it. It is far too important to just leave it and never get to know what the power of love could do for you. If you really understand its powers and abilities, when you put it into action with other tools to make things happen in a positive way in your life, you will reach happiness and success.

Therefore, I believe that a person who is capable of truly forgiving anyone is capable of doing anything this person desires to do, as long as it is positive and good for everyone and not just for oneself.

When you understand how these tools work and practice working with these tools until you can really put them to work for you, then you can't help but to be successful. There isn't anything that anyone can do about it.

Therefore, when you become knowledgeable enough with

these tools, then you've become wise and intelligent enough to be successful and prosper in any areas of your life. By this time, you've become intelligent enough to be able to truly forgive anyone, the way it should be done, with all your heart, mind, and soul, and with all your strength, as God wants us to forgive.

When we have done the proper forgiving, we realize that we feel such contentment and a peaceful feeling afterward that we do realize that the taste of forgiveness is sweet. It is actually that good, and the feeling is just that pleasantly great and rewarding. This isn't just for a few of us; it is for anyone and everyone equally. It is for anyone who is able to truly forgive.

If you have problems forgiving, I can tell you that you're not the only one with this problem. We all have these kinds of problems in our lives, but we must recognize these problems and solve them. Only then can we go on and live a more peaceful life. Myself, I certainly had my share of these kinds of problems with forgiveness in the past. My work was cut out for me just to get to the point of being able to truly forgive. It has been such battle just to overcome this problem that sometimes I just felt like giving up on it, because I didn't really understand how it worked or how I could make it work for me.

It was frustrating at times, because I just didn't know how. But after praying about it, asking God to help me with my struggle, and reading helpful books, mainly the Bible and other holy books, I've come to understand the power of these tools and how they should work together. I learned how to apply them to work together in harmony. Only after I really grasped the proper understanding of it all and came to realize the real power that was in it, then I found that it was much easier to forgive. Now that I've done it once or twice, I really felt good and at peace from this forgiveness. This feeling was so great that I wanted to forgive anyone and everyone, because the more I forgave, the better I felt about it. Well, I also knew that to be forgiven. I had to forgive or I myself wouldn't ever be free from my own wrongdoings. Therefore, the more I forgave, the more I felt forgiven. That is probably the biggest reason why I felt so good about this forgiveness. By forgiving someone else, I was also releasing myself from this bondage of not being able to truly forgive, and by not being able to be forgiven; in fact, I wasn't able to really forgive myself for any wrongdoing.

Therefore, the bottom line is to be able to truly forgive is your own freedom, peace of mind, and happiness in your life. No peace of mind, no freedom; no freedom, no happiness. It's just as simple as that. Forgiveness is a very big piece of the puzzle that is very important to deal with; in fact, it is one of the most important pieces of the puzzle, so it is not to be ignored by anyone at any time. It is a very strong universal law, one of God's laws.

Now again, I would like you to stop reading and really concentrate on this chapter. In fact, I would really like you to go back to the beginning of the chapter and read it again, because I know that you will get a better understanding of it. Reading it again will make it easier for you to put this great piece of the puzzle at its proper place, and it will also be easier for you to see the full picture of it all before you go on reading any further.

Take your time with this and don't rush. It is far too important to just rush through it for any reason.

Please stop now, and may God bless you with your studies and efforts.

We must realize the fact that when we do truly forgive someone else, especially someone that we would probably find difficult to forgive, for whatever reason, we will be truly rewarded. Forgiving the most difficult to forgive would only bring the biggest reward, because then we are just taking a bigger load off of us. We really feel light, at ease, and really happy with ourselves for our achievement with our forgiveness.

We certainly have the full right to be happy with ourselves for doing such a thing, because doing such a thing for others, as well as for ourselves, is really doing the will of our heavenly Father the way it is meant to be done, with love for everyone.

We also have to know the reason why we get to feel so good and happy about ourselves is because our heavenly Father is the one that makes us feel this way. We made Him very happy with our good deeds and doing His will. He rewards us openly just as He has promised, and we all know that God always keeps his word.

Now going back to sharing some of my own experiences with you, in some past years in my life concerning forgiveness.

At some time in my life, I called myself a Christian, and I was happy to call myself a Christian. But for a long time, I was lacking something in my life, especially in my Christian life. But being so preoccupied with my daily life, I didn't realize what it really was that I was missing. So after a while, I started realizing that it was bothering me more than I had realized. However, I still couldn't put it together, so I spoke to God about it and asked Him to show me the way and let me know what the problem was and what I could do about it. I have found that sometimes it seemed as if there wasn't any power at all in my prayers, and that made me feel sad. I felt as if I was useless and didn't have any ability to do anything that was worth doing, concerning Christianity. I wasn't happy with myself; I couldn't be happy with myself, but didn't know what to do about it.

One day I had a certain dream that really touched my heart. I was so touched by this dream that it took me about a week to finally get over it. My dream was about Jesus, and His second coming was very near. It seemed so real, and it seemed as if Jesus was upset with me. The last thing I would ever want is to have Jesus upset with me for any reason, but it seemed so real. While He was standing behind me, He told me in a very strict way, that everyone was equal and all the same and that everyone should all be treated equally.

I've decided to take a good hard and honest look at myself, and I studied myself, but I was still struggling with this problem. I certainly wasn't very happy at all with the results, and certainly not about the way I felt about it.

Again I turned to God for an answer, but this time, because I was so sick and tired of my unsuccessful attempts, it seemed that I had more faith in receiving the answer that I really needed to solve this problem. In fact, I knew ahead of time that I was about to get my answer, because I showed God an act of faith. When I spoke to Him this time, I broke down and shed tears. Realizing why, I knew that my answer was already there for me, and it certainly was there. An experience like this is something that someone would never forget.

God let me know that I didn't really have true forgiveness in my heart. Certain people had done me wrong in the past, and my words were only idles when I would say that I had forgiven those people. I was just fooling myself by trying to make myself believe that I was really free from all these burdens, and that I would be forgiven because of my forgiveness to others. I had some work to do on this matter, and God showed me how.

My heavenly Father showed me a very good book that contained the explanation about how to truly forgive others. The name of the book is "The Prayer That Heals" by Francis MacNutt. One of the best little books I've ever read.

As I've mentioned before, true forgiveness has to be done from the heart, mind, and soul, and it can only be accomplished with the power of love or it just doesn't work. Without the power of love, forgiveness just doesn't exist, for love is the power of forgiveness.

First, we have to make things right with God, with the other person, and especially with ourselves. We have to be able to visualize and recognize the goodness that there is in the other person. Whether we see it visually or mentally, it is a fact that there is goodness in everyone. Even if it might be difficult sometimes for certain people to take on such action, it just has to be done and with honesty in one's heart.

We very well know that because of lack of forgiveness throughout the entire world, we witness disputes, battles, and even wars all over the world. Every day there are murders after murders, as if murder was becoming a habit or as if it was a must to kill someone else just to make things interesting, or whatever. Because of lack of forgiveness, or lack of understanding the true definition of what this powerful word really means, and how effective it really can be in everyone's life all over the world, there is much suffering.

Well, you may call it anything you wish, but I call this

nonsense "evil wickedness." I know that I have the perfect right to call it that, because I very well know that if there isn't true forgiveness from someone, there usually is the ugly, evil disease called selfishness. As far as I'm concerned, selfishness is destruction, destruction of happiness, joy, health, wealth, and anything else good that goes with it.

The key point here is, forgive anyone if you want to be forgiven. But if you don't really understand what forgiving is or how to forgive, then I suggest that you study the word of God from the Bible and practice it. There are also very great books that explain how to forgive, what you get out of it, how well it pays off, and how good it makes you feel after you have truly forgiven someone else.

We have to realize that forgiving anyone else is getting rid of one of the most heavy burdens that anyone could carry, because we know that the harder we find it to forgive, the heavier the burden is to carry around in our lives. We just can't live happily when we are carrying such a heavy burden.

When we go through life carrying such a heavy and ugly burden, we feel miserable and don't know why. We get angry at people for no reasonable causes, and we seem to tire so easily and don't understand the reason why. We get frustrated with others and even with ourselves, and in the process; we certainly don't make ourselves loveable at all. On the contrary, we become hateful, and that makes us feel even more frustrated and angry at the world around us, but we don't understand why.

People walk away or stay away from us, because they don't feel at all at ease when they are with us. Therefore, they just stay away and choose someone else for their friend. We see others having fun and laughter, and we wish so much that we could be just like they are. We just don't realize that all we have to do is getting rid of this heavy burden that we are carrying through our lives. How beautiful life would be without this ugly burden.

Now I would like you to stop reading and really concentrate on what you've read until now. And again, please make sure that you understand the whole chapter properly before going on reading any further.

The importance of this book is much too great to just ignore it. Don't just read through it quickly to get it over with so that you can go on to the next chapter, because you may be curious and anxious to read the rest of the book to see what it is talking about, and what it has to reveal to you. Take your time, and make sure that you are patient with it. Please do it right?

Please stop now.

⌐

This chapter is so very important in your life and in everyone else's life also, especially the ones close to you, the ones you love, and the ones who love you or at least should love you. This fact could make the whole difference between joy of life and miserable and difficult life.

Forgiveness brings peace of mind, which gives us more willpower and strength to cope with the difficulties that we face in our lives. We must admit to ourselves that one of the most challenging problems in our lives is recognizing a problem within ourselves. Accept the fact and being willing and ready to do whatever is necessary to solve the problem, even if it takes disciplinary actions on ourselves and use of the tools that are called D.T.C., which we worked with in the second chapter.

We just have to remember to use some efforts and the will to make things better in our lives. We can make all the difference in the world.

Let me give you an example of how so very important forgiveness really is, and yet so many people don't realize how it is so powerful in everyday life.

Let us just imagine raising our children. Every time one of them did something wrong, we would say to this child, "Your mother and I don't forgive you, and we will never forgive you." We would do the same to all our children all the time of their upbringing.

It is my belief that these children would be troublesome. They would feel they were living in a world of hatred and would probably feel panic and anger. They would get themselves in trouble with others and with the law while they would be still in their teens. They probably wouldn't know any other way in life, and they would have to learn, as we say, the hard way. Without realizing it, they would be paying the price for the wrongdoing of their parents.

You might be saying to yourself that I am pushing it a little too far or that I am exaggerating, but I am not at all. This is reality in our lives, whether we like it or not. There isn't anything that we can do to change that.

Now let us suppose that we were to raise our children differently, with love, patience, and forgiveness, and showing appreciation for the good things that they have done and making them feel good about themselves for doing good. The results would be vastly different.

Therefore, raising children and taking care of them in these kinds of ways, is in reality, making good people, loving and kind people. I say it again that these people become successful and prosperous in their lives. It is obvious that these people grow up and live with peace of mind and happiness. They really feel and know the joy of life, and they know how to live it. They know no other way, and forgiveness plays a very big role in their lives.

These people are living deeper into spirituality than others are, and sometimes, even more than they realize. They don't really know any other way to do it, and don't even realize how blessed they are for living the way that they do. They don't hardly have to try, because they were raised that way, always in a positive way and always ready to conquer the negatives.

I really hope that you have taken these studies very seriously and studied all the chapters properly until now. It is for your own benefit and no one else's. I hope that you are keeping God in mind as you read and study, because I know that when it comes to such important learning, God will certainly help you if you ask Him. He will make it a success for you in whatever you decide to do as long as it is good for yourself and for all society.

You may find sometimes the pieces of the puzzle don't all seem to fit properly. Therefore, you have to go back and read it again, even right back to the first chapter if you need to, until you can assemble all the pieces together, see the whole picture, and get the meaning of it all, before you read any further.

I personally thank you for being patient with me until now and for being obedient, and for being willing to listen and learn, because I know that with this, your future will be brighter and you will have success in the years to come.

Please go back and read the entire book again after you've completed it.

God bless.

We have to forgive to be forgiven, and everyone needs forgiveness. Matthew 6, vs 14, 15.

Review: Chapter 11, Forgiveness

I call forgiveness the way to salvation because we can only get into heaven if we are forgiven, and we can only be forgiven if we are ready and willing to forgive anyone else that may have trespassed against us. Therefore, I believe that it would be safe to say that forgiveness is the key to enter the kingdom of heaven, and if we refuse to forgive anyone else, it doesn't matter who, then there is no hope for us.

But if you know someone that you never would have thought that you could ever forgive, and then I say it is better for you to give it another thought. Think about it very strongly, because you are not punishing anyone but yourself. Since we can only be forgiven if we can find in our heart to forgive others, then it has to be done. The harder you find it to forgive someone else but still find the strength to do it, then the reward would be much bigger then it would be if it was just an easy one.

Therefore, there is righteous and happiness in forgiveness, forgive your brother or sister and our heavenly Father will forgive you also, and it is a promise from God Himself and it can't be changed by anyone at anytime, because God's word lasts forever.

Chapter 12

Deeper into Spirituality

Now that we've studied on reality of life physically and spiritually, and all of the tools or gifts or abilities or powers as you wish, specified in this book, I believe that we should be ready to move on a little deeper into spirituality.

Now let us talk a little about Jesus' teaching, and develop common sense and intelligence, so that we can move on in a higher stage of mental development and understanding.

By putting the work that we've done in this book together with the teaching of Jesus, and being honest and serious about it, then you should be able to see the real picture and the spiritual path and most importantly to start walking upon it.

Once you've reached this degree of developing an understanding of the whole system and how it all works in such wonderful harmony, then you have become intelligent or you have received the power of intelligence. It would be difficult to find a more important power than intelligence. We know that love, faith, wisdom, and so on are very important, but we also have to realize that, without intelligence, it would be practically impossible to use the others. Only an intelligent person is capable of using any of these great powers, and only an intelligent person can become wise enough to do so.

Therefore, speaking of Jesus' teaching, we very well know that Jesus was a very intelligent person or He wouldn't have done or wouldn't have been able to do the work that He did for all of us. All the blessings that we receive from Him, and all the support from above, even though most of the time people don't even recognize or realize how those blessings come to us, and how helpful these blessings really are and why.

Through my studies and research, I have found that some people would take advantage of blessings that they have received. They didn't even realize that they were abusing such a wonderful thing that they had received from the Lord our God, but then when things are not going so well, then sometimes they even attempt to put the blame on the Lord for what is happening to them. Why does it seem that nothing can go right for them? They get frustrated and run out of patience with everyone around them, and because of their own mistakes, everyone else is paying the price, as if that was everyone else's fault instead of their own.

Sometimes it makes me feel bad and it bothers me to acknowledge these kinds of behaviors. Some people may think or even believe that they are not doing anything wrong at all. They may think that they themselves can do no wrong, and they would even be ready to argue about it. They would get upset if they couldn't have their way with others. They don't realize how much they are really hurting themselves with these kind of behaviors.

These kinds of behaviors come from lack of understanding oneself, and reality of life, as it should be understood. Because of that, then one of the most, if not the most, evil diseases that anyone could have, starts building up in a person without that person realizing it. It is called selfishness, and we already know that with selfishness, there is no true joy or happiness to be found in anyone's life.

Therefore, we, and I mean everyone of us, it doesn't matter how good or how smart we may think we are, we all should take a real serious look at ourselves once in a while. One good way to do this is to go into the bathroom, close the door behind you to make sure that you are alone, and prepare yourself. Stand in front of the mirror, and take a good look at yourself. Examine yourself in the mirror, and then look at yourself directly in the eyes. Ask the one that you see in that mirror, did you do anything good today? What did you do that was so good today? Is it worth talking about it? Do you really feel good about yourself for what you've done today? Did you do something good for others? Did you think good thoughts about others? Did you have the chance to give a good influence or to think or say something kind about the whole human race?

Did you really do any of that and was it done from your heart? And I know that for some people it is very difficult for them, to just keep staring at the one they're looking at with a straight face, and to really be honest with this person about what you are saying.

I know that it is very hard to look at yourself and lie to yourself, especially when you are all alone and speaking to yourself. Anyone who can do that would probably have to be someone that practiced it until they could face themselves, face to face, and really lie to themselves, but that would be nonsense because one would be practicing going backward in life.

But, usually, people can see themselves as they are. If there is a problem, they would be willing to deal with it, instead of just trying to disregard it and think that it will go away. An intelligent enough person knows better than to even try that, because we all know that nothing goes away unless we deal with it first, and then we can make it go away for good.

Imagine that if a person had said something wrong to someone else and hurt their feelings sometime during the day. Imagine the person facing himself that same evening and saying to this person staring from the mirror, "I was good to everyone, and I only said kind words to anyone that I was speaking to. I did this all day, and I am proud of myself for being a good and kind person all day. I really showed love to everyone and because of that I am really happy with myself."

I couldn't even imagine anyone who could do that and still able to stare at the person in the mirror. I am certain that no one could do that and keep on staring into the eyes of this person, without having to move their eyes away, because we know that lying is a shameful thing to do, and the shame makes him or her move their eyes away.

Therefore, this person won't forget this very easily. That is just what changes a person to become a better person, and after he or she becomes a better person, then he or she has the perfect right to be happy. After a while, others start finding that this person is really a nice person, and they want to be this person's friend. It sure feels good when someone else wants to be our friend. So just like the scriptures say, do to others what you want them to do for you, and all will be well with you.

Like a great song says, love your enemies, do well to those who hurt you, and live in my love. These words are very powerful, and it takes an honest and intelligent person to understand this message and to live according to it. We know that this message is also from the scriptures.

We also know that any teaching from the Bible is the best

teaching anyone could ever find and use for success and prosperity in anyone's life. When we realize that we are all in this great book of life, and there are no exceptions, everyone is in the Bible.

We also know that the great teachings of the Bible start right from the very first page and continue right to the very last page. With this, there are no exceptions, because as far as I know, every word of the book of life is a word worth reading and studying very carefully. Everyone's life story is in this book, and if you don't realize that this fact is acceptable and should be accepted by everyone, then I strongly suggest that you study your Bible. It is far too important to just ignore it, or to think of taking it up later on in life, just because we think that we are too preoccupied with our own daily routine every day.

This book of life as I really like to call it isn't only the book of life of the ancient population; it is really the book of life for everyone from the beginning of time until the end of time.

When God gave the Ten Commandments to Moses on the two tablets of stone, they weren't only for Moses and the people that were waiting for his return below Mount Sinai, the commandments were for all generations to come until the end of time. When it comes to a direct commend from our Father, God, there is no mistaking and no exceptions. It does last forever.

Therefore, if you are a little curious about it, which I really hope, you are, pick up your Bible and check it out in Exodus, chapter 20, 1-17. After you've done that, then you will realize how much you've picked up from these passages, how much easier it is to understand these teachings, and how much more you appreciate your studies and learning from this book and from your own Bible. It will also help you visualize the whole picture of it all, and it will also help you with your study on the rest of this book, especially because at this point, you are getting closer and closer to having both feet on the spiritual path, if you don't already have them there.

Now let us get ahead into the New Testament of the Bible, and get some important information from Jesus' teachings.

We know that Jesus favored teaching in parables, whenever He had the chance, and whenever it was fitting in with his teaching to put the message across, He used many parables and they were attractive and really got people's attentions.

The most popular parable that we know of is the one about the Good Samaritan, found in Luke, chapter 10, 30-37. It is a very powerful parable, and it touched and still touches lots of people. It is lasting because of the message and the feeling that we get from it. We already know that the message is to do well onto others as you would like others to do onto you. It doesn't matter the cost. There is always a great reward afterward for doing or performing a good act. To help and make someone else happy, one cannot fail but to receive from such kindness to anyone, especially if it is done from the heart with love. A great reward always awaits you for your kindness to others. It is a key to success.

Another parable that really attracts my mind also is the one of the friend at midnight, found in Luke11, 5-8. If someone comes to you at midnight and asks for food to serve to his friends because he doesn't have anything at all to give them, if you would refuse him and tell him to go away empty-handed, that would be one of the worst things you could do to anyone, and also to yourself without realizing it. But if you were to get up and give him whatever he needs for his friends that would be one of the best things you could ever do for him and also for yourself. God will reward you for helping his other child as you are one of his children yourself, and He would be pleased with you. If we do something to please God our Father, we can be sure that He will certainly reward us openly.

Elsewhere in the scriptures, Jesus taught his disciples about the bread of life, in John 6. 25-59. He taught them that He was the true bread of life, but still they wouldn't or couldn't understand what He was saying to them, even though He repeated Himself to them time and time again, so that they would grasp some understanding. Nevertheless, they still remained partially mentally blind to His teaching of the bread of life, as many of us are still to this day. Most of the time, it is because of lack of understanding the tool of listen, learn, and obey.

With all the resources that we have available to us these days, I have to say that there isn't much excuse for not understanding these great teachings that are so very important to all of us.

At the time that Jesus was here on Earth among His people, I can understand why it would be so difficult for them to be able to understand, or to find it so difficult to realize or to grasp the proper understanding, of what He was saying to them. For some reason, they were being kept blind from some of the real things, if I may put it this way, and the time hadn't came yet for them to understand everything. The body of Jesus wasn't dead and resurrected yet, and they were to see the light and understand more fully after He ascended to heaven and sent the comforter to them so that they may see and understand what He was really saying to them.

Jesus saw that they were much too dependent on Him for mostly everything, instead of putting more of their efforts in learning. They didn't understand that, with enough faith, they too could do the work that He did, and even greater work than they saw Him do. But they just couldn't see how it could be possible for them to do these things; therefore, they would just find it much easier to just get Him to do these things for them.

Jesus knew that He had to go through all of what He went through, which is suffering to death on the cross to save us from our sins, and his resurrection on the third day after he was crucified. He knew He would show Himself to the disciples, and that He had to leave the physical form of his body to go meet the Father in heaven. Only then could He send the comforter to them, which was the Holy Spirit, to be with them and in them.

We have to realize that this teaching of Jesus wasn't only meant for the people and the disciples of that time. His sacrifice and teachings are for all humanity until the end of time. Therefore, we have to realize that when Jesus was talking to His disciples, He was really talking to me, to you, and to all of us. We really should listen to Him and have obedience to his teachings. And, as He said, He will give us eternal life or everlasting life with Him in the kingdom of heaven.

Now this is a reward that couldn't ever be beaten. There is no reward ever that could surpass this reward. It doesn't matter what it is. This reward is there for all of us for the taking if we want it and if we are willing to reach out for it and receive it, but the decision is ours to make.

Verse 45 of this chapter says, it is written in the prophets, and they shall be all taught of God, every man therefore, that hath heard, and hath learned of the Father, cometh unto me.

Verses 47-51, He said unto the multitude, verily, verily, I say unto you, he that believeth on me hath everlasting life.

Verse 48, He said I am the bread of life.

Verse 49, He said unto them, your Fathers did eat manna in the wilderness, and they are dead.

Verse 50, He said unto them, this is the bread which cometh down from heaven that a man may eat thereof and not die.

Verse 51, He said unto them, I am the living bread which came down from heaven: if any man eat of this bread he shall live forever, and the bread that I will give is my flesh, which I will give for the life of the world.

We know that He was talking about giving his physical body to the world so that we could grow spiritually and have everlasting life with Him in the heavenly kingdom, where there is no remorse no pain no regret no problem, but only everlasting joy and happiness.

At this time, I would like you to stop reading for a while and really focus on what you've read in this chapter until now. I really would like you to go back to the beginning of this chapter and read through it again. Please don't try to read too fast; take your time. I ask you to have your Bible by your side and read these passages also from your Bible.

I would like to suggest that a King James Version Bible with a concordance would be a great help to you. Maybe you already have one, and if you do then you are fortunate.

But please make sure that you completely understand what you've read and are able to put all these pieces together before going any further. Don't forget to go back as far as you need to go back to make sure that you can grasp the understanding that you need.

Please stop now.

Now let us go into more of Jesus' very powerful teachings, which in my view are probably the most powerful and important teachings of the New Testament for us to study and to live by. These teachings are especially important today, with the problems of the world that we have to live with every day of our lives. They help us to cope with these problems and even prevent some of them from affecting our lives.

They are especially comforting when some loved ones are on the war field, and someone else is trying to kill them and they have to fight for their lives.

There are some that don't even have to go to war to get killed, and that happens every day all over the world. Sometimes it is just by accident, but nevertheless, people still suffer the consequences.

We know that many of times disasters could be prevented, if only people would stop and think and use common sense. It would certainly reduce the amount of accidence and killings.

It would certainly reduce the amount of problems in our society if more people would use common sense more often, and understand the reality of life as it should be understood by everyone with no exception.

This only means that there are not enough people who are willing to study and learn from such great teachings from the Bible and from books such as this very one.

The great teachings of Jesus are in reality what we all need in our lives to keep us going and to help us cope with the problems that the whole world must deal with every day. Whether we realize or recognize this fact, the real truth is, if it wasn't for the Holy Word that so many people read and study, this world would certainly be a worse place than it is now.

Therefore, if there were more people reading and studying the word of God, then the world would certainly be a better place to live in and there would certainly be fewer problems to deal with in our society and all over the world. Wouldn't you agree?

We know that Jesus was a very great teacher, and in my view, He was the best teacher and the most important person that ever lived among us. It makes no difference how you see Him, whether you see Him as God Himself or the Son of God, just like us as our brother, or the greatest prophet who ever lived or just a storyteller, or whatever. It doesn't matter how anyone sees Him, because Jesus was and still is the most important figure to humanity. He changed the course of life in humanity, and His life, death, and teaching affected the whole human race for a better life, more than any other man who ever lived.

We also know that His influence is so great that still to this day, and probably forever, there are more books sold concerning Jesus than any other books all put together all over the world. His name is mentioned more than any other name in history of mankind, since He was born among us. I believe that His name and teaching are getting stronger and stronger every day, even though there are still so many who strive so desperately to destroy or to overcome Him and his great teachings. But we know that it is mostly because some people just don't want to have anything to do with it, because they find that they just don't have the time to spend studying and learning from His teachings. But, hopefully, they will change their minds before it is too late.

Some people do understand enough to know and to want to go to the heavenly kingdom after they die, but they say that they are not ready yet. Later on in their life, they will go for it, but for now, they don't have the time. They are missing the whole point and could be missing the boat, as we say. It is really sad to see and to know this, but it is a reality in our society.

Therefore, because He is the most important and inspirational person who ever lived among us, then I for one want to follow Him and learn everything I can from His teachings. I believe that it is the most intelligent thing for me to do. I believe that it is the most intelligent thing for anyone to do. It doesn't matter who it is, we all need it so desperately if we want to succeed and live with joy and happiness in our lives.

The next chapter will reveal more of Jesus' great teachings from The Beatitudes.

God, our Father, sent His only begotten Son to teach us, with the very best of teaching we could ever receive. I have to say that His teaching certainly is no joking matter, because His teaching was done both by word and by actions, to the point of using His own body as the sacrifice for us to be saved from our sins and so that we could understand and do the will of God our Father.

No other teachings could ever surpass the teachings of Jesus, because He gave His own life on the cross. He suffered to death for us. He certainly deserve enough respect from us that we should, at the very least, study His teaching, listen to what He said, and learn from it and, most importantly, obey His powerful teachings.

We have to realize that all that He did was only for us, and not for Himself, because He certainly didn't need to suffer to death on the cross for Himself. In fact, He didn't even need to be born with a physical body for Himself, because He was already in heaven in a spiritual body. He was already in heaven, where there is no danger, no suffering, no mistakes, no problems, and no negative whatsoever, but He came down to us, put Himself in danger, and died a terrible death, just because He and our heavenly Father loved us that much.

"Let's prays Him for who He is." (These are some of the words from a song that I have written.) and for what He has done, and still and forever will be doing for us.

Amen

Review: Chapter 12, Deeper into Spirituality

I have to admit that I was looking forward to get to this part, because I always enjoy reading and talking about the Beatitudes. I always feel blessed whenever I have the chance to share it with someone else.

I believe that the Sermon on the Mount is the stronger part of the Bible, and I believe that it is the strongest teaching from Jesus for all of us that we so desperately need today.

Whenever we don't feel well, feel sad about something, or have some kind of problem, then we should just stop for a moment, relax, and grab the Bible and start reading The Beatitudes of Jesus. We would soon find that we are already feeling much better by the time that we finish reading through it. I know, I do, and I also know that it works for others, too. Just remember that suggestion, the next time something isn't going as well as you wish it to go, and you will experience this fact for yourself. You will be glad you did. Also tell friends about it so that they too can get that kind of help. It doesn't cost anything, and it doesn't hurt, either. I promise you that you will be happy that you did.

If there is any part of this chapter that you don't remember, then I strongly suggest that you go back to the beginning of the chapter, take your time, and read it again.

In fact, if there is anything that you don't remember from anywhere in this book, I strongly suggest that you start at the very beginning of the book, take your time, and read it again carefully so that you don't miss anything. Be sure that you do understand everything covered, because you really want to find the answers to your questions, and you really want to see the whole picture as we talked about before, so that you can find the right path, walk upon it with both feet, and feel the glory of the Lord. Amen.

~

With all my heart, I hope that by now, with the help of the Lord, you understand enough so that you can walk on the spiritual path with both feet. I certainly hope that you will keep on walking on the right path.

I pray that the Lord will be with you and help you all the days of your life. May the blessings of the Lord fall upon you forever and ever, Amen.

With the love that I've received from God, I love you with all my heart.

Chapter 13

The Beatitudes

Now let us go into The Beatitudes of Jesus, found in the book of Mathew. These are the passages of the Bible that I was referring to earlier. You will realize that the teaching of this book will fit hand in hand with The Beatitudes of Jesus, along with other parts of the Bible.

Before Jesus was back from the wilderness, where He fasted for forty days and forty nights, and afterward, He was very hungry and was tempted by Satan. But He refused to obey Satan, and on Satan's last try, Jesus rebuked him and said to him, "Get thee hence Satan: for it is written, Thou shalt worship the Lord thy God and Him only shalt thou serve, then the devil left Him." Matthew 4: 10.

After the devil had left Jesus, angels came to Him and ministered unto Him.

Afterward, Jesus heard that his cousin, John the Baptist, was cast into prison. He departed into Galilee, and leaving Nazareth, He came and dwelt in Capernaum, the land of Zebulon and the land of Neph'tha-lim, by the way of the sea, beyond Jordon, Galilee of the Gentiles.

The people, whom sat in darkness, saw great light; and to them which sat in the region and shadow of death, light is sprung up, and from that time Jesus began to preach, and saying, repent: for the kingdom of heaven is at hand.

Then He went walking by the Sea of Galilee. He saw two brethren; Simon called Peter, and Andrew his brother, casting a net into the sea; for they were fishers. Jesus said to them, follow me and I will make you fishers of men, and they left their nets and followed Him, and went on and found two other brethren, James the son of Zeb'e-dee and John his brother in a ship with Zeb'e-dee their father, mending their nets and He called them, and they immediately left the ship and their father, and followed Him.

Jesus went about all Galilee, teaching in their synagogues, preaching the gospel of the kingdom, and healing all manner of sickness and all manner of disease among the people, and his fame went throughout all Syria. They brought to Him people with all kinds of sickness and disease, and even some people that were possessed with devils, and lunatics, and those that had palsy and He healed them all.

Then great multitudes of people followed Him, from Galilee, from Decapolis, from Jerusalem and from Judaea and from beyond Jordon.

When Jesus saw the multitudes, He went up into a mountain, and after He was sitting, His disciples went to Him, and He opened his mouth and taught them, saying:

Blessed are the poor in spirit, for theirs is the kingdom of heaven. Matthew 5: 3.

We must realize the fact that poor in spirit didn't mean, as we say, "poor spirited," but rather your own spirit of yourself, which means humanly or self desires such as clinging to riches on Earth, whether it be money or properties, etc. But please don't get me wrong here, because we know that having money or possessions of properties. etc., is neither good nor bad. But what is bad is if you have your heart set upon your possessions, instead of upon the one that created it all. But for the sake of example, keeping our old negative habits of doing things that we shouldn't do or saying things that we shouldn't say, especially if it be something that would hurt someone else's feelings, and most importantly, negative thoughts toward anyone else.

Good and happy thoughts for all humanity are food for the soul. If someone gets rid of any negative thoughts or habits and replaces them with positive ones, that person will be blessed, and as Jesus said, "you will see the kingdom of heaven, and there will be the greatest reward possible to us."

This also comes from the power in prayer, for when we pray, we should pray attentively and seriously. To have prosperity or to be prosperous means receiving all our needs through prayers, and we know that the proper way to pray to our heavenly Father is to really and honestly communicate with Him, including the prayer that our Lord Jesus taught us so very well, which is the Our Father or the Lord's Prayer.

The only or the most powerful way of praying is, as Jesus said, directly to the Father in secret, and our Father who is in the secret will hear us and reward us openly. Jesus said, enter your closet and close the door and pray to the Father there, and we have to pray to Him directly and attentively.

This means to close your mind to the world or to anything in the world that might distract you and prevent you from being completely silent and from being able to be alone with our heavenly Father. Communicate with Him, having all your heart, mind, and soul focused on Him and nothing else. This is the only way that we can be alone with our heavenly Father and really have a good and serious conversation with Him, for Jesus taught us that we should pray in spirit and in truth and only then our Father will hear us.

The place of silence, as we know it, is in our mind, heart, and soul. Silence is power, and noise is what diffuses this power. Therefore, where there is complete silence, there is power, and the Holy Spirit is active. When we can make the Holy Spirit active in our lives, then we know that we have reached prosperity, and when we have reached prosperity, then we have reached all that we need. That's when our heavenly Father gives us all that we need, and there is no mistaking it, because that is a promise from God Himself. It is planted in God's universal law that will never or couldn't ever be changed.

Therefore, being poor in spirit is being free from anything that would prevent us from reaching our heavenly Father, meaning anything that would cause us to have our hearts upon it instead of on God.

We have to realize that if we have our heart on some possession that we may have, then we are not able to reach our Father, which is in secret and silence. Our heart would be directly to Him, it is very simple. The scriptures tell us that we cannot serve two masters, which is the difference between God and mammon. It isn't possible to serve them both at the same time; therefore, the choice is ours to make, but we have to make a choice, and we always hope that the proper choice will be made.

Let's look at the book of Matthew, chapter 19: vs. 20-22, about the young rich man. He had his heart on his riches and refused to let go of all his possessions and give it all, or as you wish, sell all that he had and give the money to the poor and follow Him. But having his heart so well bounded to his possessions, well, sadly enough, he refused the offer and walked away sorrowful, for he was willing to do almost anything necessary to follow Jesus, but when it came to leaving all of his possession behind, he just couldn't do that. His heart was far too much on his possessions, and he couldn't serve two masters at the same time. He chose mammon over God.

He walked away sorrowful, but I am sure that he wasn't or wouldn't be the only one that would do just the same. We can imagine how easy it would be to follow for someone who doesn't have anything to sacrifice, but how hard it would be for a very rich man to give up everything he has and just walk away from it all for any reason. We very well know that many people would even kill to keep their possessions. Therefore, Jesus knew very well what He was saying when He said that it would be easier for a camel to go through the eye of a needle then it would be for a rich man to enter into the kingdom of heaven. That was a very true statement, and it certainly is something that is very well worth studying from Jesus' teachings.

But, even though the Bible is the best book to study and to learn from, we still have to be careful that we do understand it the way that it should be understood, and not make all kinds of mistakes by lack of understanding it properly as it should be understood. The Bible, being the best and most popular book in the whole world, and in my view, it is the only best and no other ever even matched or could ever match it, because it is the book of life and everyone of us is in it. How could that be beaten or overcome? I don't believe that it would ever be possible.

As Jesus was teaching them, He went on to say:

Blessed are they that mourn: for they shall be comforted. Matthew 5: v 4.

Now for the sake of the meaning of the word, mourning isn't

something that anyone would want or it isn't something that anyone would enjoy, especially when we already know that our heavenly Father doesn't want us to be sad and mourn. He wants us to have joy and happiness in our lives, for our God knows very well that it isn't possible for anyone to prosper if we are sad and mourn and in sorrow.

Nevertheless, many times for many people, it seems that suffering, mourning, and sorrow are necessary; because that's the only time that someone will even think of God, when they are, as we say, at the bottom of the barrel. There is no other way or no one else to turn to, and then they feel all alone, sad, and mourn in sorrow. Then and only then, they think of turning to God for help and rescue, as it is mentioned in one of the previous chapters. For some people God, always comes last, even though He is all that we need and is always ready and willing to come to our rescue. But still people will ignore Him and don't want to have anything to do with Him.

Sometimes they think that they don't really need Him right now or yet. But because He is such a wonderful Father and He loves us so much, He never leaves us behind and forgets about anyone of us. He is always waiting patiently for us to call upon Him for help.

Our heavenly Father doesn't want to be ignored or forgotten. Because He loves us so tremendously and He is a jealous God, He doesn't want us to have any other God but Him, and rightfully so, because He is the only true God and only Him should we serve. He is the only God that has everything that we need, and that He is always ready and willing to give us whatever we are in need of. No other god can do that; therefore, He doesn't want us to get caught up with some false god and just waste our time walking in darkness.

Therefore, the message here is, mourning could be good for some people, but it is definitely necessary for others so that they can find comfort, and this comfort only comes from God our Father through Christ our Lord and Savior.

It is really unfortunate that people wait until they're in such despair and in need of help in such degree that only then they realize that there really is a true God, a God that they can rely on and reach out to and get the help that they need to get out of this terrible situation.

There is no need for anyone to go through all this kind of sorrow and suffering, but people are blind and remain blind until they fall into such terrible situation. Then they get to realize that there is really great help for them, and all they have to do is recognize our heavenly Father, and reach out to Him and ask for His helping hand. He is always waiting to help us in any way, and with anything we need.

Therefore, for some people mourning and sorrow is really a blessing to them, for they get to know God and get comforted.

Sometimes, certain people will turn to God when they desperately need Him for certain kinds of help, whether it be for money, health, or some other kind of help that they might need to get whatever they want or really need. But then, after they have received their help and they are again on their way, and they think that everything will go well for them from that time on, then again they seem to forget about God and what He has done for them, especially if it is physical wealth. But still, there are some that would never forget Him and what He has done for them, because sometimes it is a health issue and they thought or they were told that they would die and they didn't have long to live. Well, as we say, on the last straw they reached out to God and cried out to Him so desperately, and He rescued them. Because they were saved from the ugly disease called death, which they were so afraid of, some may call it a miracle, some may call it luck, some might even say that the doctor was wrong, or whatever. But the person that really received the blessing really knows what happened. This person never forgets his God and lives his life for Him from that moment on. For such people, there is no turning back from Him for any reason whatsoever. They keep receiving blessings from God and pray to Him every day of their lives because they believe that their lives belong to Him that saved them, and rightfully so. Therefore, this person has found the right spirit and won't ever want to let go of it, because this person is very well comforted.

Jesus went on teaching them saying:

Blessed are the meek: for they shall inherit the Earth. Matthew 5: 5.

First of all, before we get anywhere, we have to realize that the word meek or meekness, in the modern English translation, really has a quite different meaning from the original meaning of the word from thousands of years ago. We really have to be careful with the studying of the Bible, and I personally don't agree that the meaning of this word should have been changed. At least, an explanation should be given.

Many people that don't know this fact find some of these passages very difficult to put together and understand, therefore, the studying of the Bible can get difficult at times for some people because of these facts, especially for the new comers that are trying so hard.

The meaning of the word meek, in the modern English translation, means, mild, quiet in nature, lacking in initiative or will, etc. But the meaning of this great word in the old text, or the original meaning of it really, is something much, much different. If we just think off Moses, for example, who is known to have been the meekest man that ever lived, besides Jesus our Lord and Savior. Moses was such a meek man that we believe that He passed on to a higher plane without experiencing a physical death, and that God just transformed Him from physical to spiritual being.

Therefore, the word meek means, being able to overcoming any physical limitation, and having dominion or having control over any physical limitation. Jesus said that with the proper faith, we can do anything we want and that nothing would be impossible to us, as long as it is good. Therefore, only a meek person would be able to accomplish these tasks, as Moses and Jesus did. There have been others also who were meek enough to be the real servants of God, but not to the same degree as Moses and Jesus were.

There is always much more explanation that could be given on a topic as such, but I believe that this information is sufficient for the reader to grasp the proper understanding of it.

Earth is another word who's meaning some people seem to have difficulties with understanding. The word earth, from the teaching of the Bible, doesn't necessarily mean the earthly globe that we live on, but it means manifestation or expression that is the result of a cause. It is the mental state of knowing the result of something that already happened or even knowing the same result of something that will happen before it happens. True faith certainly plays a big role in it.

Therefore, blessed are the meek: for they shall inherit the earth really means anyone who is willing to listen and learn from the word of God and obey His commands is meek and will inherit the earth. A meek person is developing the proper understanding and intelligence to the point where there is enough faith to be able to conquer any negative influence and replace it with positive influence, whether it be heath or wealth, it doesn't matter. This is when a person has control over his or her life the proper way, and there is nothing anyone can do about it. This is what God our Father meant when He said that He gave us dominion over all. With the proper and enough faith, we can do anything we wish to do with no limitation because we have dominion over all. This is probably one of the biggest, if not the biggest, blessings that anyone could receive from our Heavenly Father. Therefore, we could say that inherit the earth means receiving the same ability to do anything we want as Jesus did, and we already know that this is a true statement because Jesus said so. If Jesus said, that's good enough for me.

And after these teachings, Jesus went on to say:

Blessed are they which do hunger and thirst after righteousness: for they shall be filled. Matthew 5: 6.

Righteousness is one of the key words from the teaching of the Bible and in everyone's life, because the meaning of this word in the Bible is what everyone needs to reach prosperity. As we know from the previous chapters, we all need prosperity to be able to communicate with our heavenly Father and to get through the gates of heaven. Therefore, this word is by all means more powerful than people realize it to be.

One of the problems in society is that people don't really understand what the word stands for or what it really means, and how so very important it really is for everyone. It is very sad to know that so many people have so much difficulty understanding the teachings of the Bible, because of the lack of understanding the true meaning of so many powerful words that are so important for everyone.

Therefore, it isn't very hard to read a book, but it is quite different to really study it. The real meaning of all the words that it contains, this is the very reason why I am persistent on "listen, learn, and obey," because it is the answer to most of our problems, especially when it comes to obedience. It seems that people want to shy away from it, because especially nowadays, people like to do whatever they want to do or whatever they feel like doing, and nothing else seems to matter because they lack the proper understanding. Because of this fact, they go through life never knowing what they really have missed that was so precious.

Now the meaning of this word righteousness could mean something bad for some people, but it can also mean everything to others. If we just think for a moment about someone who is self-righteous, it is someone who thinks of himself as better then God Himself, if he even believes that there really is a God at all. Or he thinks that he really doesn't need God to control his life for him because he can do that himself and that everything will be just fine without anyone else's help.

Unfortunately, a self-righteous person of this kind really, as we say, completely missed the boat and doesn't even realize what really happened because they are too preoccupied thinking of themselves better than anyone else. They don't really have time for anyone else or even many times don't have time to spend with God our Father, which is the creator and controller of all that exists. But for some people, they don't realize this fact, because they really don't take time to think properly about all of the other people all around him and even of God.

Therefore, someone that is self-righteous is really someone that, in reality, doesn't even think properly or don't have the ability to think properly about the whole universe and all that there is in it and the purpose of it all. Therefore, there really isn't any great enough future to speak off for these people, because in reality, they are lost in their own self-righteousness and don't know how to get out of this situation. Some don't even want to get out of such situations because they really believe that they are happy just the way they are; therefore, unfortunately, they don't even realize how far they are off the mark. But some do realize some truth about it all but, just like the rich man that refused to get rid of it all to follow Jesus, they just find it far too difficult to do and would rather hang on to their own self righteousness and hope they will be forgiven and that everything will be OK. But that's not the way it works, it is very easy for someone to fool themselves that way, so please don't let yourself fall in a situation like that one, be careful with everything you do or think.

Righteousness isn't necessarily what a person will do in action, but rather what a person thinks, because the way a person think is the way the result will come out. It is the thinking that makes the results, as we say, "as within so without." We know that proper righteousness is really right thinking, thinking good thoughts. If you want good to come to you, then you have to think good thoughts at all time. If you want prosperity, then think thoughts of prosperity and believe that you will receive prosperity, and you shall receive it. If you want healing, then think healing thoughts and believe with all you heart, mind, and soul that you will be healed, and you shall be healed.

Therefore, good thoughts will bring good results and bad thoughts will also bring bad results. It is very simple, it is a universal law and nothing or no one can do or change anything about it, and no one should even try in any case.

Everyone should think good thoughts, not only about their friends or family members, but also about everyone and everything in the whole universe because it is all good, it is for everyone, and we all are brothers and sisters. We all live in the same world, and the real truth is that we all need each other. Whether we realize this fact or not, it really doesn't matter, because that is the way it is and was meant to be, and that's the way it will stay. As our Lord said, love one another as I have loved you, take care of each other, pray for each other, and we can't forget that He said love your enemies and do good to those who hurt you and live in my love.

These are very strong words, and we have to understand what these words really mean. We also have to really think good thoughts for everyone before we really can do that, even though it seems to be so difficult sometimes to obey these commandments. But obedience is the way to salvation. There isn't salvation without prosperity, and there isn't any prosperity without right thinking (righteousness). We very well know by now from studying this book that it takes a wise and intelligent person to be righteous for the right reasons and to reject anything else that may come in the way of right thinking.

We all know that probably the most difficult thing there is for us to do would be to change our thoughts, always changing negative thoughts to positive thoughts. We know that it is a very difficult one to do, but it is more difficult for some than it would be for others. Nonetheless, it has to be done, and with enough practice, it certainly can be done. There is no doubt about it, because we know that there are lots of people that has already done it, and received their rewards.

Therefore, anyone who hungers and thirsts after righteousness shall be filled. So when we pray, we should pray attentively for righteousness, asking our Lord to give us right thinking or to help us think right at all times. With the proper attentiveness and believing with all your heart, mind, and soul, our Lord will answer our prayers and help us, and we shall be filled.

Especially right thinking while praying will bring right results. Anyone that can do this is sure to win, because it is God's promise to all of us. It doesn't matter who we are or what we have done in the past, because God forgives and helps anyone at anytime. We must speak to Him with a sincere heart, and really mean what we say to Him. We know that He cannot be fooled by anyone at anytime, and He cannot be mocked.

I believe that it is a good practice, before praying to God, to prepare ourselves with our plans, meaning to put our plans in the proper order before talking to Him to make sure that we know what we will be talking about and to make sure that we really mean what we're about to say to Him. It is a very good practice to get in that habit, also, because it would make your prayers much more meaningful and especially stronger, because as we know, God is always willing and ready to listen to a sincere heart and will always reach out and help anyone of His children who have a sincere heart. Therefore, I say, prepare right thinking about getting your plans in order, and as Jesus said, enter your closet and there be all alone with our Father which is in the silence, and speak to Him that hears you, with an open heart, mind, and soul before talking to Him. Then you are certain to be ready for Him and He also will be ready to answer any of your prayers as He said He would.

Therefore, proper preparation takes right thinking, right thinking brings prosperity, and prosperity certainly brings good results. That isn't just for some of us, this is for everyone, and there is no exception. We are all the same in the eyes of God; we are all his equal children, and He has the same love for everyone of us.

Therefore, we have to realize and recognize the fact that we cannot think one thing and produce another result at the same time. It is not possible for someone to think a negative thought and do something good and positive at the same time, or vice versa. So what we express on the outside always comes from the inner thoughts and beliefs. That universal law could never be changed, which only means that it is the only way to go or to be.

Therefore, we know from reading the book of Genesis that God said that He gave us dominion or power over everything, meaning dominion or power over our thoughts, to think as we should or as we will, so we make our lives by the way we think.

Jesus tells us that we have no power or control over outer things, because the outer things are the consequences of what goes on in the secret place, or in the silence, which is our thoughts, and with the right thoughts (righteousness) nothing is impossible to us, we shall be filled.

The root of the problems and troubles in the world for humanity is the fact that people do think poverty, sickness, and all kinds of negative things that could harm someone, whether it be physically or emotionally, or sometimes it could be some kind of destruction to someone's belongings, etc. As mentioned in

244 Joseph C. Plourde

previous chapters, we really are the creators of our own problems because of the simple fact that we lack right thinking.

Think health, and you will be healthy. Think joy and happiness, and you will have joy and happiness, or success and prosperity, and so forth. Therefore, if you want to control your life, first you absolutely have to control your thoughts or you just don't have control of your life. As far as that goes, you don't even have control of anything or anyone, because you then don't have dominion or power over anything, even your own life. I have to say that it would be very sad to see, and even worse, it would be a very sad thing to experience.

We also should realize that one very evil thing that so many people struggle with, and it seems that they can't control it, is fear. This is really something that people make a reality in their lives. They think a bad thought, and they fear that it might happen to them. Because of the influence that they get from that kind of thinking, all they really do is create a negative energy for that problem, enough that this problem becomes a reality for them, and then they try to fight it or get rid of it after they have created it.

Fearful thoughts are very powerful, especially if you give fear power with your thoughts. Therefore, if you can "turn the table around," as we say, and get rid of these negative influences by practicing your thoughts and get to the point that you've gained control of your thoughts, then you've got control of your life also. Then you're reaching the stage in your life where you have dominion over all, which means your life and all there is around you that concerns your life. Also whatever is good for others, and we can't forget that at that point, faith becomes very strong and that is when nothing is impossible to you; you really have dominion over all.

Therefore, if you want dominion over all, as God said, then keep thinking God thoughts with dominion over all with Him, and make a habit of doing so every chance you get or as often as you can. Don't let go of it, and it will come to you, because we have to realize that the word God is the most powerful word in the whole universe.

Each time that the word God is being said by someone, then this person is never the same afterward. Every time this word is spoken and you really pay attention to the pronunciation, you can actually feel the energy surrounding you and through you. It is a true fact and whenever anyone wants to experience this feeling, well just try it; concentrate on it for a while, and then when you're ready then say the word God. Wait a few seconds, and repeat it again while you are concentrating on it. Again, you will realize that it does change you and your attitude toward this great word or name, as you wish.

This is a very good and rewarding practice. It does bring good results to anyone that practices this task. It gives you a very good and warm feeling because you feel the presence of God in you and surrounding you. It would be difficult to get a greater feeling than this one, because whenever someone feels the presence of God in and around him or her, then this person really feels secure and at peace and one would wish to keep this feeling forever. They really never experienced such great feeling before, and they don't want to lose it. I suggest you try it and experience this feeling for yourself, and if for any reason you have problem getting this great feeling, then you need to concentrate more on it and don't give up and you will get it.

Now, going back to having dominion over all with or from right thinking, we know that it isn't the easiest task to accomplish, but it certainly can be done. Therefore, if you've tried for a short time and it almost seems as if it would be difficult to reach your goal in this matter, please don't ever give up. It is far too important for you. All you have to do is keep calling on God to be with you always as you work on it and He will help you if you're patient and persistent enough, God don't give up on you. Therefore, why should you give up on yourself or even on Him, common sense says keep going.

If the problem persists, then I strongly suggest that you stop for a moment and really think deeply. Is there anyone that you haven't forgiven yet? Is there anything that you may have done to someone else who you've never approached and asked for forgiveness? Have you ever approached God sincerely and asked Him for his forgiveness for thinking bad about someone else? Have you even had some bad thoughts about some of God's creations? Well, if it is the case, then I strongly suggest that you think again, because you will not get anywhere this way.

First things first. Forgive and be forgiven, and don't hide or even try to hide anything. God knows and sees everything, no matter what or where or who it may be. You have to clean it up and mainly clean yourself up first, and then you have freed yourself from anything that could prevent you from accomplishing your tasks. Look straight ahead and reach out for more goals in your life. You definitely have to be and feel completely clean before you can even attempt to reach any of your goals in your life, and remember that right thinking will take you there, and help you reach your goals.

Do not remind yourself of the mistakes that you've made

in the past. In other words, don't live in the past for the past is dead and gone. We all have to live for today and look forward to tomorrow. We don't look back, because in life, we have to look ahead and reach into the future. This can be done, but it isn't possible to reach into the past and live in the past; therefore, don't waste your time looking back in life, but just keep looking into the future for your goals to reach. With Good righteousness, you will not have to worry or fear anything.

After making certain that you are absolutely clean with yourself and with others, you have peace of mind. We need piece of mind before we can do anything right, or before we can even have right thinking. Make sure that you didn't leave anyone behind that you know you should deal with, be strong and honest about it, and you will have all the rights to be happy with yourself for what you've accomplished just by doing that. We do understand that sometimes it can be a difficult task to conquer, but remember that the more difficult it is to accomplish, the bigger the reward. Be strong and honest about it, and you will find happiness, success, and prosperity that can only be found with honesty and peace of mind.

Jesus tells us not to be discouraged if we can't accomplish everything all at once, if we find that it comes too slowly, or if we are too slow at what we are doing about it. If you are not progressing at all with it, then your prayers are not right; therefore, I suggest you spend more time thinking about if there could be any jealousy or resentment left in your heart, or hatred toward someone else. Check to see if you have any resentment toward a religion or any organization, or if it might be personal or political. It doesn't matter. Please make sure that there is absolutely nothing left undone, so that you can be absolutely free from any negative that could be lingering on in your life. Do whatever is necessary to reach your goal in finding peace of mind and peace of heart, and then you can walk side by side with the Lord and become victorious. Righteousness will take you there.

Therefore, if we strive for righteousness. We shall be filled with happiness and prosperity.

And Jesus went on with his teachings saying:

Blessed are the merciful, for they shall obtain mercy. Matthew 5: 7.

Merciful and mercy are some very strong key words that we find in the Bible. Like forgiveness, loving, patient, helpfulness, and so forth, these words are all key words. More words than these are all over the Bible. These words are all so very important that they are parts of our living; therefore, they certainly are not to be ignored. For myself, I really see merciful or mercy somewhat as "reap what you sow." Be merciful to others at all times, and we shall obtain mercy.

Now, we really have to be careful here with this, because we know that many people are likely to get fooled with these actions, for the simple fact that some might do some good deeds to someone else from the goodness of their heart, but others will show a good deed to someone else, but it is just for the fact that they will receive something in return, and for no other reason whatsoever. This isn't being merciful in any way, nor have mercy on someone else; in fact without realizing it, they are not even being merciful to themselves.

We must realize that we cannot think one thing and do something else at the same time, so we cannot pretend to be merciful to someone else with outer actions if it is meant to be for self profiting. That is called hypocrisy, and hypocrisy in my view is something very evil. There is nothing good that could ever come out of anything evil; therefore, we have to be very careful how we do a merciful act, because it is very easy for anyone to fool oneself while trying to fool someone else.

Hypocrisy is a very sneaky disease that can come and creep up on us without ourselves realizing it. If we don't take time to examine ourselves once in a while, then before we know it, it has got the best of us already. Sometimes it can be difficult to get rid of it because it has already taken control of us and our lives, but this can certainly be overcome, we are constantly honest with ourselves and with anyone else also. As long as we remain truthful and honest with everyone about everything, then the evil disease of hypocrisy doesn't have any chance whatsoever to come creeping in because the door is always closed to it, and there is no room for such evil.

We could say that hypocrisy would probably come from another evil disease called selfishness. Those two diseases belong together, and they fit hand in hand with each other. If we give them the chance or the power over us, then we would have problems to overcome. These are evil diseases; once they are set in and start acting as a destruction in our life, so I say please be on your guard at all time and stay safe by being honest with yourself and with the whole society.

Being merciful doesn't necessarily mean to be merciful in action or with external actions. As important as action is, being merciful in thoughts is the real major key action to the real proper merciful action for anyone to take. Being merciful in thoughts certainly brings true mercy in external actions, because as mentioned before "as within so without" means what we produce in our mind, we also produce with our outer actions.

Therefore, if we occupy our mind with good or merciful thoughts for anyone else as often as we can, then we are certainly on the right path. We certainly don't want to get off that path, because it is the path to glory and it is the right path. In fact, it is the only path that we would want to be on no matter what the cost is.

As you read, just stop for a moment and reflect your mind on the meaning of these words: "Be Merciful, and you shall Obtain Mercy." This is a wonderful and very powerful wording. We can't help but be touched by the meaning of these powerful words. I can't speak for anyone else, but for myself, I can say that when I focus my mind on the meaning of these words, I really feel good inside. I feel as if it gives me strength, and I feel that I am being guided the right way or am on the right path; therefore, I certainly feel blessed with strength and peace of mind and happiness that I feel that would last forever. After getting this kind of feeling, I certainly don't want to ever let go of such feeling.

When we exercise this kind of action often enough, then we get to the point that it seems as it just becomes a habit and we certainly enjoy it. By that time, we surely have gotten rid of lots of problems and difficulties in our lives. That helps us live a happy life with peace of mind and prosperity, and there is no turning back for any reason whatsoever. Life is wonderful, everything in the universe is beautiful, and the power of love is in action. We want to cling to it as if we never want to lose it for any reason.

This, to some people, may seem like a lot, but all this and many more blessings come from mercy or being merciful. This is obtaining mercy for our good deeds of being loving and merciful to anyone because everyone needs mercy.

We have to realize that, even though this may sound very

wonderful and beautiful, the truth of the matter is that nothing or no good profit comes without good works. It takes good thinking in planning, dedication, and efforts to produce anything worthwhile. Without works, nothing good happens. Even God had to work when He created everything and everyone, and then on the seventh day, He rested. But his works were wonderful and everything was according to his plan, and it was all good and it was all done for us all.

Therefore, as powerful as God really is and still He did the works, His work certainly wasn't as simple as ours is. All that He created, all the laws that He has made, and all He put in proper order, was so that everything operates in the proper fashion and in harmony with each other, and that includes humanity. All we have to do is keep everything in proper order and keep it living in harmony as it was meant to be.

But still as a weak nation, we find everything too difficult to handle, even though God told us that whenever we need help, all we have to do is call on Him and He will be right by our side, ready and willing to help us anytime, anywhere. All because He is such a merciful God, and He will not let anyone or anything get in his way. All we have to do to get Him to help us is speak to Him, pray to Him the proper way so that our prayers can be answered as Jesus taught us.

If you show me that you are merciful, and I really see that it is coming as a direct action from your heart, then I will personally reward you by being merciful to you also, and probably more than the mercy that you've shown me. This is how it is, not only with a few or only with friends or loved ones; this is the way it is for the whole society. All humanity is alike, and it doesn't matter what we think of someone else, it doesn't change the fact that we are all the same, all in the same family of God, for we are all brothers and sisters. There is nothing that anyone can do about it. Whether some people like it or not, God made it this way, and speaking for myself, I love it and appreciate it just the way it is. I wouldn't want to even attempt to change anything about it even if I could.

I have to admit that I enjoy this kind of living most of the time. I enjoy working with others, and talking and communicating with others, even though we don't always agree on everything we say or do. We know that we are not perfect and, humanly speaking, we know even ahead of time, even before we start talking to each other, that there might be some disagreements; therefore, there shouldn't be any reason for anyone to get upset or angry with anyone else. It seems kind of, as we say, childish.

It is easy enough to recognize a merciful person in the crowd, and usually, it would be the one that is the most quiet, who only speaks when he would have something kind or merciful to say to the others. Many times, it would be mentioned by someone else about this person being the smartest in the bunch, because he doesn't say anything unless he has something good or smart to say. But then you realize that, in a few minutes, this kind of attitude is already forgotten by the others, instead of trying to keep the flow of the kind words going, as if they are not interested in this kind of merciful talk. They slip right back into their old habit of being unkind about or to others. Sometimes it is by talking about someone else as if they are not even there to speak up for themselves. That also certainly gives a bad impression to others and can put a bad influence on others, who aren't as smart as they think they are. They are sure to be far from being intelligent and wise, and this is certainly not being merciful to others. Therefore, that makes me wonder how they could obtain mercy as their reward for being kind and merciful to anyone else. Well, then I realize that we have to pray for these people for a better change in their attitude toward others, so that they can also get to the point where they too can obtain mercy, and speaking for myself I would certainly like to see all my brothers and sisters get rewarded with a well deserved mercy.

Anyone of you who does understand the true meaning of the words mercy and righteousness has already received your blessings from God and you have overcome the difficulties that were in your path. I say to you that you should be prepared and ready at all times to help anyone that would need your help, as you needed help when it was you who was struggling. I am sure that you know as well as I do that there is absolutely no excuse for refusal to help anyone at anytime. We very well know that you have a duty to perform and to have your blessings grow, and then you have to perform your duty with an open heart and free will. You have a brother or sister to save, and there is no time or room for selfishness or refusal to reach out and help him or her, no matter the cost.

I am saying these words because I have seen too many people who claimed to be Christians and claimed to know everything that they needed to know to serve God, but at the same time, they claimed that they didn't have time to reach out and help someone who was calling out for help. It's especially disappointing if someone claims to be such good preacher, and then he tries to teach people how to obey God and walk with God all of the time. Well, someone who dwells in the world full heartedly, is likely to refuse to be merciful to anyone anytime he feels like it. What I can say about that is simply that I am glad that I don't live in such a person's shoes, because as Jesus said, they will find their rewards, which means on the street-corners or wherever they can be seen, or recognized by people. There will be no room in the kingdom of heaven for them, and it is very sad to see and to know this fact, because there are many of them.

Therefore, if you are one of them, I say please turn around and take a good look at yourself and do whatever is necessary to save yourself. Get walking on the right path, be merciful to anyone at anytime, and exercise this work until you have gained your power and abilities to walk with God at all times. Then you would be ready to teach others about salvation and about the great blessings that they can receive from our heavenly Father. But until then, you can't teach anyone about mercy or righteousness, or even about true love, if you don't even do the works yourself. It is hypocrisy, and where there is hypocrisy, God would turn away and not have anything to do with such an evil thing.

Please don't get me wrong here with this kind of talk, because I am simply stating the truth as I feel that it should be stated. My aim here isn't to hurt anyone's feelings, but simply to open the eyes of anyone who is walking toward or on the wrong path. I feel that it is my duty to help in any way I can, and this is exactly what I am doing. I certainly hope that you understand, take my advice, and put it into practice before it is too late. Act while you still can rescue yourself from your own condemnation, and find hope, peace of mind, and true happiness in your heart, and find the proper mercy that everyone should want and seek.

Therefore, these laws are not only for just a few of us, or just for certain people, they are for everyone equally, and there is no exception for anyone.

Jesus continued teaching them saying.

Blessed are the pure in heart: for they shall see God. Matthew 5: 8.

These words "pure in heart" are some of the most favorite and powerful words in the Bible. We all know that God is the most favorite and powerful word in the Bible and in the whole universe, because God controls the whole universe and everything that's in it in perfect accord and harmony.

Now to see God, in my view, would be something that most people would want, but we have to realize that God isn't in any form as we are. We couldn't see Him in any physical form, but nevertheless, without realizing it, we do see God in the works that He does every day of our lives. But the sad part is that, because of our lack of understanding, we oversee God's activity in our lives; therefore, in our own ways of seeing the reality of our own lives, we are unable to see the real reality of life as it should be seen. We miss the real purpose of it all and the reason why it was created the way that it was, and the one that created it and for what reason.

We know that there are people that like to say things like; well, I didn't ask to be in this world so why did someone bring me here? Well, this is someone who really lacks understanding of the reality of life and all its glory. This is certainly someone who really doesn't see God at work at all, God's work every day of their lives. This is a very sad situation for anyone to be in.

Therefore, we can understand why we cannot see God unless we are pure in heart. Before we can be pure in heart, we have work to do on ourselves before we can even imagine of seeing God. The only one who can get to see God as He is, is the one who lives according to God's will. It doesn't matter the cost or the practice they have to put into it, to reach the point of being pure in heart. In reality, this isn't as difficult as people see it or think it is; it is as easy or as difficult as we make it, and it is mainly done either way by the mental habit of thinking. Then to bring out the good deeds in physical actions, for example, think good for the whole society, including yourself and our heavenly Father, and be always willing and ready to reach out and do whatever is necessary to please God by loving and helping anyone at anytime. Practicing this kind of loving kindness certainly brings a person on the way to see God.

Therefore, the statement in this beatitude couldn't be closer to the truth. We also have to realize that it is a promise that with a pure heart we will see God.

We understand very well that God doesn't have a corporeal form. We know that it is not possible to see Him in an ordinary physical form as we see a human being, because if it was so, then He would be limited. God knows no limit. Therefore, to see God is in a spiritual sense, and yes, we will see God if we become spiritually inclined enough to reach the point in our lives where we can have a pure heart. Only the pure in heart will enter the kingdom of heaven, and only the ones who will enter the kingdom will see God.

In heaven, there isn't any physical form as we see each other here as we are, but we will have a spiritual form, if I may put it this way. If a spirit is invisible, then I believe that only spirits would be able to see spirits. By putting it this way, you might find it easier to understand the spiritual world. You should be able to understand how we will get to see God.

But to my understanding, in reality, we do see God every day, but we don't realize it because of the spiritual perception that we lack so sadly in our human lives. Therefore, even though God is always among us, we still don't have enough understanding to be able to see Him. This is what I call living in darkness, or blindness, because of the lack of understanding the spiritual life, which is really the real true life.

We have to realize that while living a physical life, we only live for so many years. But in the spiritual world, we live happily forever, for eternity, and in everlasting joy with our Lord where there are no difficulties, no problems, no hard times, no sorrow, no limitation, but only everlasting life with peace, harmony, and happiness with everyone. There we will surely have the door opened to us and see God.

Therefore, pure in heart is physically to get to see God spiritually, but to see God in heaven doesn't mean to see Him somewhere in the sky or some unknown place, because heaven is right here, right now, all around us, at all times. God being in heaven simply means that God is always with us and all around, and best of all, He is in us. But many of us don't even know or realize this fact. As Jesus said, "I in Him and Him in Me, Him that created and control everything for the whole universe and everyone in it and no one is left out, therefore, blessed are the pure in heart, for they shall see God" This is one of the richest and beautiful sayings in the entire Bible.

This short statement from Jesus contains so much more then we realize. Jesus didn't have to do so much talking to get to the point. He could sum up meaningful messages in such short sentences.

We know that there are many people who are pure in heart, and also throughout the past, there always have been people that were pure in heart, many of them throughout history. We will choose Moses for one of the best examples we can use from

history. Moses was certainly pure in heart, and He very well knew
what being pure in heart really meant, and to Him, it meant
nothing less than knowing that God was the only power, the only
cause of being or existence, existence of the universe and all that
it contains.

Moses understood that God had control of his mind. In fact,
He even understood that God was the power of his mind, heart,
and soul and that everyone was living in God's world. That to
succeed in his life, he just had to do God's will and he wouldn't
ever fail but only succeed. Because of the faith that he had in his
God and the tremendous amount of love that He had for Him,
he was pure in heart because he knew that his God was the only
cause or power that he could live with, that God was his very
existence and that he couldn't get anywhere except through Him,
by Him, and with Him at all times. According to the Bible, we
know that Moses saw God and met Him face to face. Therefore,
seeing God really means seeing Him as the only cause or power
of existence, and anyone who understands this fact, obeys it, and
lives according to it is pure in heart and will surely see God.

And Jesus continued teaching them saying,

Blessed are the peacemakers: for they shall be called the
children of God. Matthew 5: 9.

This beatitude contains a very powerful message that needs
to be properly understood by everyone, because this message
contains the key to real peace or serenity. We have to understand
that real peace or serenity is nothing less than peace of the mind
and soul, and only with real peace or serenity can anyone be a
real peacemaker. Only a true peacemaker can really communicate
with our heavenly Father. As was mentioned before, one has to
enter his closet and close the door, to find real peace and quietness

to commune with our Father, which is in secret, with an opened heart, mind, and soul. Then we can reach serenity and only then can we become a real peacemaker and only then can we get to see God.

Anyone that wants to properly concentrate and meditate on God and spirituality needs serenity, or I don't believe that it would be possible for anyone to have a total focus on God and spirituality, unless one has real peace of mind or serenity. We have to realize that the only time that we can truly communicate with God is when we have only total focus on God, and absolutely nothing else as if nothing else existed.

This is true peace, and anyone that has true peace is certainly a peacemaker, and therefore, is a child of God.

We also have to realize that prayers are the key to power to overcome anything negative that may come to hurt us or damage our lives and prevent us from reaching our goal in our lives. We also know that the only powerful prayer is concentrating on God and communicating with Him with a clear conscience and peace of mind and soul, or serenity, because that is when we know for certain that God really hears our prayers. That is also when we get and understand his answers. That's also when we can see God as He really is. Once we experience this true fact, then we just like Moses, want to communicate with Him all of the time, because of the great feeling and the reward that we receive from recognizing how wonderful it is to live with Him all of the time, and even just from the realization of how great it is to know for certain that we are really the true child of God.

Therefore, not only believing but knowing that God the Father has accepted us as His true child is probably the best feeling that anyone could have as a reward for recognizing who or what He really is and for being able to truly communicate with Him the proper way. I pray that everyone will get to know how to communicate with Him every day of one's life and receive the greatest feeling that anyone could ever get.

We also have to realize that every time we pray, we change our being and our habits; we become a better person. Whether we realize this fact or not doesn't matter, because even if someone is praying without true peace of mind or serenity, that person will still change to a certain degree, even though it may be a small amount. But it is still a true fact that every time we pray, we do change for better. But when we really pray with serenity, then we certainly do change in a larger degree because our prayers are so much more powerful than they are without serenity, because we are praying with an opened heart, mind, and soul. Therefore, our communion with our heavenly Father is pure and true, and that is the only way to pray to Him, if we really want an answer from Him, and to really receive his great blessings that we need so desperately every day of our lives.

Therefore, when we reach this stage in our lives where we have real peace of mind and soul, or serenity, then that's when we have dominion or power over all, as God said in Genesis, the first book of the Bible. He said that He gave us dominion over all, which meant that we shall have no limitation. Jesus also said this when He said that if we have the proper faith, then there would be no limit to what we could do. All the works that He did and even greater works we could do, and to my understanding, Jesus said it that's good enough for me. That settles it.

With a pure heart, clean soul, and serenity, we are peacemakers, and therefore, children of God. That is a promise from God Himself, and we know that His word will never change.

Jesus kept on with his teaching, saying to them:

Blessed are they which are persecuted for righteousness' sake: for theirs is the kingdom of heaven. Blessed are ye, when men shall revile you, and persecute you, and shall say all manner of evil against you falsely, for my sake. Rejoice, and be exceeding glad: for great is your reward in heaven: for so persecuted they the prophets which were before you. Matthew 5: 10-12.

What a wonderful, powerful, and moving statement this is for us today, and probably one of the best, if not the best, teachings that we certainly need to study and to well understand.

This statement here might very well startle some of us, but we do have to realize and understand that the real truth is that we are our own persecutor and no one else is. We very well know that we are persecuted by our own thoughts and no one else's thoughts. Being persecuted for righteousness, or right thinking, is for example, someone who strives to have good positive thoughts all of the time and struggles to keep only good and positive thoughts in mind all of the time. But there are always bad and negative thoughts that come and try to take the place of the good and positive ones. We always must combat these negative thoughts and really don't want to have anything to do with these negatives, so we strive to always have good thoughts. But, there is always interference with the negatives, and most of the time, that really is a fight or struggle to conquer these negative influences.

These negative influences were planted in us by no one but ourselves. Now we are the ones that have to struggle to overcome or conquer these negatives that we have planted in our own mind to begin with. But sometimes, it could also be because of something that we might have seen from someone else, or something that might have happened to us from someone else. That could have been something that we didn't know anything about or something that we didn't have the opportunity to do anything about it until it was too late, but nevertheless, because we are the ones with the struggle for right thinking, or righteousness, we are the ones who are persecuted for righteousness and no one else. But after saying this, we also have to realize that if we had our own heart, mind, and soul in the proper harmony, then in reality, we wouldn't have all these struggles, because we would have forgiven our trespassers immediately. We would have realized that this person didn't know any better, otherwise he or she wouldn't have done whatever was done; therefore, our real duty is to release this person from his own persecution, by simply forgiving this person. By doing that, we are also releasing ourselves from our own persecution.

We have to realize that releasing ourselves from persecution in this very case is the real fact that by forgiving someone else's trespasses against us we also can be forgiven. To really be able to forgive ourselves our trespasses against ourselves and against others, then we really have peace of mind and soul, at least on this particular issue; therefore, we wouldn't have to struggle with any negative thoughts on this matter, because we would be happy with our deed at this time. There would only be good and happy thoughts going on in our mind, and there would be no room for bad and negative thoughts. I have to say that one of the biggest parts of becoming righteous or having righteousness would be to get rid of any resentment, jealousy, hatred, or fear of anything or anyone, and to make absolutely sure that there is nothing left to uncover or to deal with, because we want to have a clear mind, a clean soul, and an opened heart at all time. Before we can even try to conquer the bad and negative thoughts that cross our mind all the time, we have to clean ourselves properly and completely.

Many of people like to act as if they really are righteous, but anyone that knows or understands what righteousness really is automatically knows that this person is only fooling himself and no one else. This really is a waste of time and effort, and anyone that acts this way really needs prayers so that this person can get to see the true light. Seeing this and praying to better this person is bringing ourselves closer and closer to righteousness, because the more good deeds we do for anyone else, and even for the whole society, the clearer and clearer our mind, heart, and soul become. Therefore, we don't have so much to struggle with before we can reach righteousness.

Here we also should realize that righteousness, or being righteous, is in reality opening the door to the kingdom of heaven for ourselves. Therefore, if we are persecuted for righteousness' sake, we will inherit the kingdom of heaven. Well, again I have to say, I believe that it is certainly something worth reaching for, because we all know that there is absolutely nothing that compares to this, and there is absolutely nothing above or beyond the kingdom of heaven.

We do realize that for some of us sometimes, it isn't an easy task to just turn the other cheek, because whenever someone else does or says something against us, immediately as a bad habit we think of getting back at this person. We do this until we have the chance or the opportunity to think about it, and as soon as we think of righteousness, immediately we change our thoughts for much better thoughts. This is when we realize that we were about to persecute ourselves again over what someone else has done, and we know that it's worth it. The price is too much to pay for this nonsense; therefore, with a change of mind and an opened heart, we decide to forgive this person and pray for him or her to see the real light someday soon, according to our Father's will. If it be today, tomorrow, or the next day, it doesn't matter, because we all know that prayers are never lost or wasted.

It doesn't cost anything to pray for anyone else, but we have everything to gain. Whether we realize this fact to be true or not, it is a reality and everyone should by all means realize and recognize this as a true fact in everyone's life. The only ones who don't understand this are those who never study anything about the reality of life. But it is never too late to start, and a very good start would be for anyone of us who understand it to pray for these people so that they too would get to understand it for it is such high degree of importance in their lives as well as in ours. Again, praying to better someone else is simply bringing ourselves closer and closer to the kingdom of heaven's door, and at the same time, we are helping a brother or sister to walk on the right path and this is the path to the kingdom of heaven.

Let's just stop and think for a moment about how great and how joyful it would be when we get to heaven for everlasting glory to see our brother who also made it there because of our loving kindness and prayers that we shared with him while we were still in the physical world with our struggles. We still found time to save our brother or sister, and because of that, it will be the reason why we will be there forever lasting life, where there is only happiness, harmony, and glory with our Lord Jesus Christ.

Therefore, when we find right thinking or righteousness very difficult to attain because of a strong negative influence or a strong temptation to hold onto some negative thoughts, whether they be because of ourselves, some bad situation, or even someone else, and it seems so difficult to have control of our own mind, then we are being persecuted for righteousness' sake. To us, it is a very strong blessing because of the simple fact that it is when we are really and rapidly advancing, especially spiritually.

We should remember here that Jesus Himself was very strongly persecuted, with all kinds of attempts and temptations, but He overcame all of what did come to Him and overcame all kinds of evil that tried to make Him join the worldly way of living instead of doing the great duty that He came here to do for all of us in setting us free from all the evils of the world. He overcame all, so that He could present us with all the great teachings that He could deliver with all the best of his ability, and all that He has done was only because of the amount of love that He had for all of us. No one could ever teach anything, anytime, and anywhere as great as Jesus did for us, because His teaching was beyond any other teaching that anyone on Earth could deliver. His teaching wasn't only verbal but also physical, to the point of suffering to death by the crucifixion on the cross. Still He never gave up and kept his duty just as He said He would and the cost didn't matter to Him because He was determined to do whatever He had to do to save us. He did exactly that, and now it is all up to us to do whatever it takes to follow his path, and as we all know it is the path to glory as it is promised to us if we follow Him.

But we can't forget about all the great heroes who were persecuted for righteousness, and anyone who has studied the Bible would know who they all are. These people we have to respect very much so, because whether we realize it or not, these people have helped pave the way for all of us because they are part of history, according to the Bible. From studying the Bible, we know they are a great help for us to understand what the Bible teaches us, and some of these people even gave their lives because they wanted to be right with God and nothing else really mattered to them. Some of them had their lives spared by God because of the great faith that they had in their God; therefore, He spared their lives and made them very great in the Bible. They helped make history and we have learned lots from their willingness and ability to conquer the negative that was surrounding them. For them to do what they have done, they needed to have a pure heart, and peace of mind and soul, to be able to conquer fear, hatred, and resentment that could have been from the ones that wanted to hurt or kill them, the ones that were persecuting them for righteousness. I believe that it would be safe to say that these great faithful people have inherited the kingdom of heaven, and that they have seen God face to face or at least have seen God's angels doing His work as they were being saved and their lives were spared from the enemies.

Therefore, if anyone says all manner of evil against you to hurt you for any reason, whether it may be because they are jealous of you, they despise you, or for any other reason, it doesn't really matter what the reasons are, the fact of the matter is that we have to forgive them and pray for them, for they don't know what they are doing. They certainly don't realize how much they are hurting themselves. That goes for anyone who likes to spend his time talking about someone else, and laughing and making fun of someone else every chance he gets. We usually call these people hateful, but in reality, we really should feel sorry for these people, pray for them, and ask God to forgive them their trespasses, even if that wasn't meant to be done against us. If it was done to a brother or sister, then it is always our duty to perform this task, for the simple reason that if our brother or sister is getting hurt, then it becomes our business or our duty to see to it that this person or these people stop doing this kind of evil nonsense. Therefore, it is our duty to forgive them and ask God to forgive them, and mainly to pray for them so that they see the true light and lose this evil habit that they hang on to just because they try to find satisfaction or better feelings to satisfy their evil jealousy or their evil selfishness, or whatever the reason they are doing some evil deeds. Therefore, someone that understand enough should really be ready and willing to help these people in the worst way.

They too are brothers or sisters and they certainly need our help, and it is our duty to help them out of these ugly, evil bondages that they are stuck with, and knowing that the sad part of it is that they don't even realize how bad this is. They don't even know how to get out of this situation, because they are living in darkness or in blindness. Therefore, we have to help them open their eyes and see the true light, or open their mind and help them understand what they are really doing. We must help them find a better way or find better things to do, because they obviously need help before it is too late. We must help them while there is still time for them to start walking on the right path, and remember that each time we perform a task as such, in helping a brother or sister, and then we are automatically bringing ourselves closer to the doors of the kingdom of heaven. We are doing the will of God, and God is very pleased with anyone of his children who is doing what He wants us to do. In this way, we are called the sons of God; therefore, the gates of heaven are opened to us.

We have to remember that it is really a great blessing to be persecuted for right thinking or righteousness, for we shall inherit the kingdom of heaven where there is everlasting joy and happiness for everyone. There isn't any other place but in heaven that this kind of living can we have and enjoy for eternity with our Lord Jesus Christ.

If we would just think for a moment how short this life here on Earth really is compared to everlasting life, then we would soon realize that it is just a glance of the real life in heaven. From realizing all of this, then we can't help but understand why it is such great blessing to be persecuted for righteousness' sake. It is simply because that makes us or help us to get on the road to heaven, therefore, after realizing how short this life is, it seems as if with some efforts and some practices for just a short time, and already we have made our way to the kingdom of heaven already, and that's just the way it is with life. May God bless you with "right thinking" (righteousness).

⌐∽

At the ending of this book, it would be wonderful for everyone to say "The Lord's Prayer."

I pray to God for His blessings upon you, with love, success, and prosperity.

Amen.

Quiz

Now I would like to give you some questions to answer. These questions will help you find out for yourself how well you really did with your studies. I am convinced you will be happy with your own results.

The answers are at the end of the book. Please be absolutely honest about taking the quiz, and you will be happier with the results afterward. Sometimes it is tempting to take a little peek, but try not to do it, and after all is said and done, you will be happier with yourself. Please take your time. Don't be too anxious to get to the end or to consult the answers.

There are spaces below each question for you to use; therefore, feel free to write in those spaces. Use a pencil if you want, but first of all, have faith in yourself and go for it.

I pray for God to help you with your decisions and with your learning.

1. My first question is very easy: What is the most powerful gift received from our heavenly Father?

Love

2. Name five of the most powerful tools that everyone should use in their lives.

3. Who was the person known as the father of faith, according to the scriptures?

4. What was the most difficult command that God ever give to Abraham?

5. Who was the first person that dealt with God face to face, according to the scriptures?

6. What is the best thing next to love, according to this book?

7. What is the most evil thing that anyone could possess, according to this book?

8. What was the great ability that God gave to all men after He created man?

_____

_____

9. What is the first of the Ten Commandments?

_____

_____

10. What is the fourth commandment?

_____

11. What is the sixth commandment?

_____

12. What is the eighth commandment?

_____

13. What is the last commandment?

_____

_____

14. What was the biggest miracle Jesus performed to prove to the world that His teaching was really the truth and nothing but the truth?

_____

_____

15. What did Jesus say would be very profitable to us if only we have some of it?

_____

_____

16. Where is the best place to go to pray to God?

_____

_____

17. What would be the best kind of teaching to others without forcing them to do what we think would be best for them?

_____

18. What are the three tools that work very well together to help us become successful, according to this book?

_____

19. How long do people usually wait before they will call upon God for help?

_____

20. What will be the reward for someone who is pure in heart?

_____

Fill-in-the-blanks Exercises

1. In the book of Genesis, God said_____ make _____ in ____ image, after _____.

2. He also said ___ them have _____ over the _____ of the ____.

3. And the Lord God_____ unto_____, and ____unto _____, Where ____ thou?

4. And the Lord said unto _____, come thou and all thy_____ into the ___; for thee have_ seen righteous before___ in this generation.

5. And _____ was ___ hundred years old when the _____ of _____was upon the _____.

6. They and every _____after his_____ and all the_____ after their _____.

7. And____ ____unto _____, and to his ____with him, saying, and I behold, I establish my_____ with you, and with your___ after you;

8. And _____awoke from his_____, and knew what his younger___ had ____ unto him.

273

9. And Abraham was_____ years old and_____ ,when he
was_____ in the _____of his _____.

10, and the _____appeared unto him in the _____
of _____: and he sat in the tent door in the____ of
the_____.

Now let's get directly to the book of Mathew.

11. Then Joseph being_____ from _____did as
the_____ of the _____ had _____him and
took unto him his _____.

12. Now when Jesus was born in Bethlehem of Judea
in the days of Herod the king, behold, there came wise men
from the east to Jerusalem.

13. Then the devil _____ Him up into the holy city, and
_____ Him on a _____ of the temple.

14. For verily I say unto you, Till _____ and _____
pass, one jot or one _____ shall in no wise pass from the
_____, till all be _____.

15. _____, and be exceeding glad: for _____ is your _____
in heaven: for so _____ they the _____ which were
before you.

16. Follow me, and I will make you _____ of _____.

17. _____, for the _____ of _____
is at hand.

18. Get thee hence, _____: for it is written, thou shalt
_____, the _____ thy _____ and him only shalt thou
_____.

19. But Jesus said unto him, _____ me: and let the _____
_____ their _____.

20. Why, are ye _____, O ye of _____ _____?

21. The _____ truly is plenteous, but the _____
are few: Pray ye therefore the _____of the_____, that he will
send forth _____ into his _____.

22. For _____ shall do the _____ of my _____ which
is in heaven, the _____ is my _____, and _____, and
_____.

23. A _____ is not without _____, save in his own
_____, and in his own _____.

24. Then Jesus answered and said unto her, O woman, _____
is thy _____: be it unto thee even as thou _____, and her
_____ was made _____ from that very hour.

25. Then Jesus answered and said, O _____ and _____ generation, how long shall I be with you? How long shall I _____ you Bring him _____ to me, and Jesus rebuked the devil.

Questions from this Book

26. What is the main topic of the teaching of this book?

_____.

27. What does this book aim to teach?

_____.

28. The first chapter talks about something that seams so hard to find or so difficult to get. What is it?

_____.

29. What makes you frustrated because you can't grasp it?

_____.

30. What do you believe you will find in this book?

_____.

31. After studying this book, what is it that you would have put all together?

_____.

32. What is the first thing that anyone must do before even trying to walk on the spiritual path?

_____.

33. Why should this book be taken so seriously?

_____.

34. By studying this book, you will find some very important tips that will help you with your what?

_____.

35. Why is the author so happy about this book

_____.

36. What is it that the author didn't want to scare you with?

_____.

37. If we want to live in happiness with everyone in the whole universe, what must we have in our lives before we can find this happiness?

_____.

38. What are the two major things we must do and have to get out of a bad situation?

_____.

39. In the first chapter, what is the only way to survival?

_____.

40. What was the very important thing that the author did before he even started writing this book?

_____.

41. When someone is in deep trouble, what is considered the wrong way out?

_____.

42. What kind of thinking does it take to bring good solid results?

_____.

43. What must a person do to build up strength and acquire the will to keep on going to reach goals?

_____.

44. What is it that God doesn't want us to live with or to live in?

_____.

45. What is so difficult for any individual to do to himself to better his life?

_____

_____.

46. Who is our worst enemy?

_____.

47. What happens to someone that can't or refuses to understand the truth about reality of life?

_____.

48. Why it is that sometimes it is so difficult to find the problem that we have to put up with for so long?

_____.

49. Who is the real creator of all the problems that we have to struggle with in this world?

_____.

50. Sometimes if we stop for a moment and take a good look around us and especially at ourselves, and realize how we think and how we should think about what is real in life, then what do we get to realize about ourselves?

_____.

51. What is the very great gift that everyone have received from God all equally, and yet so few people are fully willing to share it with each other equally and free of charge?

_____.

52. If anyone don't understand some of the words and what they really mean, for example, will, and what it really stand for, and faith and what it really is and how powerful it really is, and wisdom, and how important it really is to understand it properly, and so forth, then what should a person really do to get the proper understanding of these great words?

_____.

53. Name three of the great holy gifts given to us from our heavenly Father.

_____.

54. When someone is willing to share love and happiness with anyone else, then this person is surely to become what?

_____.

55. We can't, or shouldn't even try to, force anyone else to live their life the way we want them to live it, just because we think we know better. Therefore, what is the better way to show them?

_____.

56. What is the proper way to approach a person who seems sad and in sorrow, a way that avoids him refusing our help?

_____.

57. How many times should a chapter be read before moving on to the next chapter?

_____.

58. When is the time when God is unable to help us?

_____.

59. Who should we share good will with?

_____.

60. Why should we share all that is good in this world with everyone equally, without exception?

_____.

61. Why should a person read the same book more than once?

_____.

62. What is the key word for people to change themselves to become a better person?

_____.

63. What is the worst thing that anyone wants to face?

_____.

64. What is the main thing to do to develop wisdom and intelligence?

_____.

65. Before anyone even think of walking on the right path, we certainly have to have the proper "what" of ourselves?

_____.

66. What is it that we shouldn't do to others, but we certainly need to do it to ourselves?

_____.

67. What did Jesus have that was so remarkable?

_____.

68. When do people develop intelligence?

_____.

69. What should be done with a child that is a good thinker?

_____.

70. Why is it that we really have to be careful with when giving advice to someone else especially to a child?

_____.

71. What is it that we have to do before giving advices to anyone?

_____.

72. Can we honestly say that intelligence is good for everyone, and why or why not?

_____.

73. Why does the author want the reader to stop reading for a while and focus on what is already read, what is the main reason behind it?

_____.

74. Why is it that the author prefer that the readers uses their Bible along with this book?

_____.

282   Joseph C. Plourde

75. Who should we have by our side to help us with our studies?

_____.

76. What is the reason why the author is not quoting all of the passages from the Bible to you?

_____.

77. What is the key for anyone to reach their goal in their life?

_____.

78. What does an intelligent person seems like to be compared to others in many occasions?

_____.

79. In everything we do it should be done with what?

_____.

80. Who should we thank for our success?

_____.

Conclusion

I certainly hope with all my heart that you've enjoyed working in this *Both Feet on the Spiritual Path*, and I certainly hope you did well with your studies, especially if you've used your Bible along with this text.

I have tried to do whatever I could to make this work as easy and as enjoyable as possible. At the same time, I've worked hard in designing the text in a way that would allow you to get the best out of it. I really hope that you did and that you are now able to clearly see the whole picture and that you are able to walk with both feet on the spiritual path, with joy, harmony, and happiness.

Now my real desire would be to know that you've achieved great results and that you've really learned greatly from this study. Mostly, I'd like to know that you are happy about your study and your success from it all.

If you've really succeeded with your work, I am very happy for you. You have every right to be happy with yourself, and to be proud of yourself and with God for your achievement. I am proud of you, but most importantly, our heavenly Father is proud of you. He will reward you openly, with all kinds of blessings that He holds in His storehouse.

I really believe that working with this book, seriously and honestly, is probably the best thing that you've done. By buying this book while looking for success in your life, and finding the answers to your questions, so that you could find better ways to succeed with whatever you were trying to achieve.

My heart is with you, and I certainly wish you the best results in whatever you do, and whatever goal you set yourself to reach, and I ask God to be with you at all time and bless you with great blessings, so that you live a prosperous and happy life for all the years to come.

I have to tell you that it is always a great idea, after a while to pick up your book and read through it, as a reminder or a renewal of memory, just to keep in touch with the feeling of happiness and success. I know that by reading through it again, you will be surprised about how much you will learn from it again, because I know that more time you read it the more you will learn from it, and I hope that *Both Feet on the Spiritual Path* will always help you.

May God bless you in all the years to come, and make you successful and prosperous.

I love you with all the love that I receive from God, and I'll keep you in my prayers.

Yours Truly
Joseph C. Plourde

Answers to Questions

1. Love
2. Patience, Love, Forgiveness, Practice, Common Sense, Concentration, Meditation, Discipline, Good Thoughts, Control, Integrated Thinking, etc.
3. Abraham
4. Sacrifice his only son as a burnt offering.
5. Moses
6. Faith
7. Selfishness
8. Dominion or power over all
9. Thou shalt have no other God before me
10. Thou shalt not take the name of the Lord in vain, for the Lord will not hold him guiltless
11. Thou shalt not kill
12. Thou shalt not steal
13. Thou shalt not covet thy neighbor's house; thou shalt not covet thy neighbor's wife, nor his man servant, nor his ass, nor anything that is thy neighbor's.
14. Resurrection
15. Faith
16. Enter your closet and close the door so that you can be alone with our Father
17. By action

18. D.T.C.
19. When they get to the bottom of the barrel, when there is absolutely no other way.
20. They shall see God

Answers to Fill-in-the-blank Exercises

1. let, us man, our, our , likeness
2. let, dominion, fish , sea
3. called , Adam , said , him , art
4. Noah, house , ark , I , Me
5. Noah, six, flood, waters, Earth
6. beast, kind , cattle , kind
7. God, spake, Noah, sons, covenant, seed
8. Noah, wine, son, done
9. 90, nine, circumcised, flesh, foreskin
10. Lord, plains, Mam're, heat, day
11. Raised, sleep, angel, Lord, bidden, wife
12. Bethlehem, Judaea, Herod, Jerusalem
13. Taketh, setteth, pinnacle
14. Heaven, Earth, tittle, law, fulfilled
15. rejoice, great, reward, persecuted, prophets
16. fishers, men
17. repent, kingdom, Heaven
18. Satan, worship, Lord, God, serve
19. follow, dead, bury, dead
20. fearful, little faith
21. harvest, laborers, Lord, harvest, laborers harvest
22. whosoever, will Father, same, brother, sister, mother
23. Prophet, honor, country, house
24. great, faith, wilt, daughter, whole

25. faithless, perverse, suffer, hither
26. the truth about reality of life
27. put both feet on the spiritual path
28. the answers to your questions
29. the proper understanding
30. the answers to your questions
31. the full picture of life
32. honesty with oneself
33. because it contains the truth about reality of life and the understanding of it all
34. physical and spiritual development
35. because he has the opportunity to offer his help to so many people all over the world
36. by making it sound like it takes lots of work
37. live in harmony
38. pray and have faith
39. keep faith in yourself and in God
40. asked God to bless him with his work
41. the lazy way out
42. good integrated thinking
43. keep thinking good thoughts about your goal at all time and don't give up
44. struggle
45. take a good look at oneself and deal with it
46. our own self
47. he or she remains in darkness, or live in blindness
48. because it is in us which is too close to see it or to recognize it

49. ourselves, humanity

50. how often we contradict ourselves

51. Love

52. study the Bible

53. Love, Faith, Wisdom, Intelligence, Happiness, Joy, Knowledge and many more

54. successful

55. by action

56. with a true smile and tenderness and loving kindness

57. as many times as it takes to properly understand it

58. when we refuse Him

59. with everyone

60. because it is completely free and it is God's will that we do so

61. to get more knowledgeable about the book if it is a good book to learn from, and to get more intelligent

62. honesty

63. punishment

64. listen, learn and obey

65. control

66. tell them how to live their lives, but tell ourselves how we should live ours

67. intelligence, wisdom, knowledge and so on

68. at birth or even before

69. help him with his mental development

70. because it could be very harmful with a wrong

advice

71. really think about it to make sure that it is a good advice to give

72. intelligence is good for people that are willing to use it for the good of society, and not just for oneself

73. so that you can really put the puzzle pieces together properly one by one so that you can really see the true picture of it all afterward

74. so that you can study the Bible at the same time, and to prevent any doubt at all from the reader and that you can have peace of mind as you read through it

75. God

76. because he wants you to learn your Bible as it is so important, and he doesn't want to make it too easy because you wouldn't learn as well

77. persistence

78. luckier

79. with the power of love

80. our heavenly Father